IN THE 7TH YEAR

Volume II

The past is written.

The present exists.

Don't keep the Future Waiting

Mitchell Ritter

FROM A FRIEND

New York has the reputation of being a very isolating city where everyone is too busy, too pre-occupied, and one might even say too selfish, to show more than a fleeting interest in others. This book reveals how that has turned out not to be the case: Mitchell Ritter reaches out and engages others, like me, in spontaneous explorations of human existence from which he has created these poems that reflect his observations.

But, back to the beginning.....

Our story began some two years ago. As I made the early walk with my dog Henry in Central Park, as is my daily custom, I noticed Mitchell sitting on his rock on a hill in the middle of the Park every morning, with additional hill-sitters accumulating in his vicinity. We started talking about dogs (he has two rather large ones), and before I knew it, we were friends.

I had assumed this was an unusual encounter. Most people one meets in public places are on their way to somewhere else. But over time the group started to grow as we became a collection of people from very different backgrounds, with the only apparent links being dogs, the hill, and conversation with Mitchell.

From random encounters, we found ourselves forming a group, looking forward to meeting each morning, and noticing when someone was absent. It became apparent that the gravitational force of Mitchell's personality was quite simply drawing others into his orbit. He is the unofficial "Mayor" of the hill, so designated by silent, slightly mocking, consensus - not by authority, given or sought.

Being myself a student of human behavior, I watched how this spontaneous collective became a group of friends. The active ingredient was someone sincerely interested in other people. Mitchell doesn't listen awaiting an opportunity to kidnap the conversation and talk about his own preoccupations. Rather, he asks intriguing questions, clearly -to deepen his, and the other person's understanding of the subject at hand, whatever that may be (and there are many "whatevers," not the usual "How Are You's?")

When I asked him about this energy, he responded by saying "How else can one learn if not by asking why?" In fact, a most unusual approach today when few are really interested in looking beyond the immediate and the obvious.

In casual conversation, he conveys no sense of making judgments. In fact, his interest appears almost objective, where finding an answer is far more important than determining if anyone was "right" - sadly the aim of most conversations. He makes the distinction between "observation" and "judgment." The former is about sharing one's personal experience, the latter is about making broad generalizations (He is very much a stickler for the meaning of words).

Listening and learning from each other: how's that for something different? This is not to say Mitchell is without passion for the things that he cares about and which can become animated, though never acrimonious or intrusively personal. Indeed, many of his values are exposed in these poems, offered for the reader's reflection.

Perhaps some of Mitchell's native curiosity and a deep concern for others has been honed by the many years he has spent living in different cultures. Forced to integrate, he had to let go of many of basic assumptions acquired in his native New York, assumptions we rarely, if ever, question as we continue to live our lives in our native surroundings. A complementary explanation might derive from his wide-ranging education and training, living in the colliding worlds of psychology and philosophy often simultaneously.

We have become good friends in the true sense of the word, though our conversations may take an annoying (for some) psychological turn, given this is our shared professional, and probably personal interest as well. I have learned to trust him, something he embraces as an honor without ever seeking to pry. And I believe he feels the same way.

Written in a style he attributes to Dr. Seuss –yes, he of *Green Eggs and Ham* and *The Cat in the Hat*, among others. Deceptively, they appear simple,

almost naïve and innocent, this book emerges as a follow-up to his previous work – <u>Six Years</u> – where the wonder of rhyme first revealed itself to him as a means of joining the rational and the emotional, to obtain a richer, more complete, yet nuanced understanding of our world.

Poetry is obviously not a wildly popular art form – the days of Shakespeare when such language was much appreciated lie behind us - though it is experiencing something of a comeback. I believe this is due to poets abandoning the painfully personal, almost idiosyncratic, and returning to Shakespeare's model. Indeed, it has often been said that to truly understand the human condition, one must read Shakespeare. I think this is what Mitchell is talking about, for as long as there have been humans walking this earth, there have been certain universals, and the study of these holds the key to understanding ourselves as both individuals and a species.

Harkening back to the somewhat forgotten classical view that humans haven't changed all that much over time, even if our circumstances have, Mitchell seeks to remind us of the astounding insights garnered from careful observation, open- minded reflection, and incredible leaps of intuition, all serving as the foundation for what we believe we know in an art/science/philosophy, still very much in its formative stage. They also indicate where every reflection should begin – at the beginning. Starting in the middle may be expedient, but more is lost than gained.

Reducing the human mind to a matter of neurochemistry and wiring is one of Mitchell's favorite complaints, on which he rarely tires of expounding. We forgive him, for his is a rather solitary voice these days when we have abandoned a bit of our humanity in favor of pure biology.

These poems reflect what I have described above: *curiosity, caring, concern, commitment,* and, perhaps a surprise to those skeptics out there), *clarity* – yes, even we psychologists indulge on occasion. . If you seek any of these five "C's," or all of them, spend some time on these pages. Pick one, any one, and start there. Let your unconscious take the lead. This work is not intended to be read cover to cover. Rather, enjoy your stroll through a world of deceptively innocent rhyme, where things matter, people matter, and the problems of existence everyone faces are taken seriously, as they should be. It might be a step towards some of those values of which we are so much in need.

So there you have it - my experience, my understanding and my friendship for Mitchell.

Enjoy this buffet of thoughts, reflections, aspirations and hopes for the future, for all our futures. I did. And on occasion, when I need a breath of fresh air, I still do..

Judith Rosenberger, LCSW, PhD

New York City

September 2017

ACKNOWLEDGEMENTS

First of all, I would like to thank all of you for letting me and my rather innocent observations and reflections into your world. I write, perhaps as we used to, not just to communicate events, but to use language for its real purpose – to formulate our thoughts. Supporting that is a preoccupation with those matters which we all share –the universal – avoiding scrupulously the excessively subjective. It is so easy to get lost in oneself these days. Every comment, and there have been many, has brought me something of value. How else do we learn?

Then, there is Dr. Judith Rosenberger (and her husband, Ernst) who I met by chance, and am glad I did. Judith applies her analytical skills to introduce me with the clairvoyance and generosity, and the poems, to those fortunate enough to actually read her "Notes From a Friend."

And finally, if you get a sense that this is a critique of today's values, I believe it is more than that. A critique is a rational analysis – mostly mind. Observations, if that is truly what they are, combine more than that. They should – and hopefully did, include a fair dose of the heart.

One thought you might want to retain. People often accuse those who offer a point of vue of being judgemental – not a popular epithet. And that can often be the case. Negativity has gained great currency of late and there will a heavy price to be paid for it.   But there is a very important difference between observing something, reflecting on it, and judging it.

One reflects humility and open mindedness. The other tends towards the dismissive and the close-minded. Think about that next time you are engaged in any conversation. One will bring you new information, a better understanding of your conversational partner, and through that, possibly even a sense of empathy.   For you to be right, does the other necessarily have to be wrong?

And with empathy comes caring – for someone, something greater than oneself. There is indeed a serious shortage of it.

Notes From the Author

Though every poem reflects something deeply personal in my experience or that of those I have had the good fortune to know, they are neither biographical, nor autobiographical.   While remaining completely authentic in their message, I felt it appropriate to respect the privacy of those who played a part in the stories these poems represent.

The style remains **Seussian**, i.e. childlike, innocent, cautionary and inspirational, without falling into the trap of platitudes or pre-baked solutions. This is perhaps a "self-help" book for the curious. As Jung said it the best….."The more one looks outside, the more one dreams. The more one looks inside, the more one awakens."

So if you feel stuck at a time and place of your life, if you don't see the way forward, believing you have tried and exhausted every possible avenue, you will discover you have much company. But because this is a universal problem for many, indeed most, perhaps what others have felt and experienced will provide you with a new way of looking at yourself, with a new perspective which, by its very nature, points to a way forward.

I write poetry, though I am no poet. A contradiction? I don't think so. Poetry is the language of the heart, of the unconscious mind where rhythm and substance combine to weave a tapestry of reason and emotion. When the two combine, they produce a level of understanding and creativity hard to encounter elsewhere. I picked it up quite by chance, never reading much poetry, and writing even less. But when the juices started flowing, it imposed itself on me, and suddenly, I could hardly keep up.

Try it. You might even like it.

One final thought. As I've mentioned, I write about what experience, trying to incorporate it into some larger understanding that hopefully becomes ever more coherent and meaningful. That being said, I am more than aware of the limitations of my perceptions. Which is why I encourage everyone to reflect on whatever may have made an impression, and if you would be so generous as to share your thoughts with me, you would broaden my perspective to include yours, and hopefully, together we will have gotten that much closer to what I think everyone in their own way seeks – some form of wisdom.

To do that, feel free to contact me via my website at the following:

www.analyticalpsychologynyc.com

There is also a blog on that site where I comment more specifically on issues relating to my practice – a very rich source of insight provided by those who do me the honor of sharing their lives with me. There too, I would very much appreciate your thoughts as well.

And if this book is your first exposure to my writing, there are two more books available on **Amazon.com/ebooks/MitchellRitter**

"Mr. Hide's Progress – or Why People Often Make the Wrong Choices"

And

"Six Years – A Concentrate of Life – Volume I"

INTRODUTION

THE 7TH YEAR - VOLUME II

September 2017

After the surprising reception of Volume I (Poetry? Really?), here I am again. What more could I possibly have to say one might ask? There's certainly a poem somewhere in here that addresses that.   To answer more directly, this past year – In the Seventh Year - much has happened which reflects not only the world around us, but how it reflects who we are today.

Why would I have anything new to contribute? My years abroad alone don't qualify me – lots of people travel overseas. One thing, however, that I find lacking here in the US is perspective – the unavoidable necessity of seeing things from more than one point of view which the bi-cultural experience imposes.

I'm not talking about living in a city like New York where there is a tremendous amount of diversity. The dominant culture is still an east coast version of America. I'm talking about being alone in a world where everything is different, where every circumstance is fraught with the possibility of a misstep. Where one feels ill at ease, gauche, at each reference one feels compelled to talk about how things are at home – as if anyone was interested. The message is clear: "You are here now so forget about home and learn how we do things here.

"Challenging in the beginning, but if embraced, it becomes a bit like having two eyes instead of one. A single eye can be sufficient when everything is familiar. But the visual world acquires depth and nuance with two. If evolution were to be truly benevolent, it might at some point equip us with a third or even a fourth one, though where to put it might be a problem difficult to resolve.

And there is also the necessity of having to learn a "foreign" (that term often makes me laugh, as it is so egocentric) language. There is the lesson in humility which learning a language imposes, where even the most intelligent people often come off as sounding like idiots, incapable of expressing their higher thoughts with the few words they possess and easily mangle, badly put together and pronounced – at least in the beginning. But once a certain ease develops, language provides the structure and tools to see the world through the eyes of not just the language, but it's structure, it's logic, and the fundamental assumptions each culture has which guides so many of its choices and its development.

There are concepts, thoughts, assumptions which simply don't exist in every culture as reflected in its language. Translation, however expert, always loses something of the original, and introduces something different in the new iteration.

And there is also the magic of words, for the are the tools with which we construct our minds. They require thought, rigor, reflection and precision. Used loosely and they breed ignorance and confusion. Used with the care any fine tool deserves, they can raise us up to heights we didn't know existed. And they can keep us honest for words misused will ultimately betray those who have spoken them. And finally, they allow us to transcend every dimension by conveying to any and all who are so inclined that which we can barely comprehend.

And finally, being a psychologist I benefitted doubly as I studied clinical psychology at the Universite de Geneve where Jean Piaget did his groundbreaking work on cognition, and depth psychology at the C.G. Institute in Zurich.

Think about it. One very small country, two monuments of the study of the human mind – one strictly scientific, focusing on the development of intelligence in children, and the other, ignoring the rigors of the scientific method to step outside the rational to see the world through the entire range of our capabilities. And yet, I believe they scrupulously ignored each other and their respective work, as their lives and careers did overlap.Studying both simultaneously, I would navigate back and forth between Geneva (French) and Zurich (German and English), taking courses on cognitive development (Piaget) and the marvels of the unconscious mind (Jung). It might have been a difficult challenge, even a dissociative one where I could have been forced to choose. But why choose when one can make that extra effort and have them both. I was lucky enough to find some way to do what neither could do – marry their exceptional contributions together, for what are we, if not beings in the process of becoming, navigating the conscious world through our intelligence, constructed bit by bit, from our earliest childhood onward and trying to comprehend the efforts and energies emanating from the unconscious to bring us balance, understanding and wisdom.

And starting by looking behind the obvious to start to understand how the human psyche, both conscious and unconscious, work together to bring richness, creativity and balance to our lives.

The perspective thus gained has become my principal currency. Jung's view of the unconscious is not something occult, even magical. Rather, like religion, culture, art – all manifestations of the unconscious – it is all metaphorical, the preferred language of the unconscious. When seen thus, the true nature of the Swiss psychologist emerges. Here was a man deeply human, deeply rooted in his very concrete, pragmatic, earthbound culture. There is mystery only for those who choose not to see.

No one holds the key to another's salvation for the factors are too many and more often than not, hidden or disguised, escaping our observation. What we can do, what I strive to do, is to show each individual that how they look at themselves, their choices and their lives is the result of many forces – internal and external – the latter too often the result of an environment that prefers to impose its demands on the individual before understanding their true nature and richness. This doesn't mean one favors a permissive approach, for children emerge with little need for or understanding of structure. Yet it is that very structure which will form the skeleton on which everything one comes to learn and know will live upon. Interiorizing these restrictions without questioning the appropriateness and degree of psychological amputation, people deprive themselves of much of the true weatth they possess. To learn to see oneself from a different perspective allows one to find solultions where one thought there were none. To find the strength and courage to attempt that which they forbade themselves, and to start to understand and reintegrate in a more differentiated and evolved form, all those things that were cast off. It is these very things that hold the key to all creativity, without which our world would be much impoverished.

No one holds the answers to another's riddle. To claim such a capacity is a serious lack of humility, if not humanity. Two people confronting life's challenges can never have the same answer. But in understanding quite simply how we got from there to here opens the door to being able to start getting from here to wherever it is we need, where we want, to go..

What is life if not a series of challenges that, if we have the wisdom to see it that way, requires us to constantly reexamine the ways of the past and search for new solutions for the future. As a child of the 50s, I grew up in a period of great optimism. Even if all the promises of that bright future with flying cars and such have not been kept, there was always be room for optimism. Without it – and we are seeing some of the effects on our society today – without something new, some goal, some project to pull us forward, the future we might want will struggle to be exist.

Yet in its infinite wisdom, and at time inscrutable neutral;, Life will most certainly dictate a new course. I wonder only if we will have the intelligence and maturity to embrace it.

Welcome to the Seventh Year – the year when the pure searching ended and the reconstruction began.   Not surprisingly, I started with an examination of the lay of the land and its inhabitants. Like Volume I, I would recommend not reading these poems as one would a work of fiction. Rather, let your intuition, your unconscious (whose purpose is to provide a deeper, more universal and meaningful point of view, designed to compensate for the unavoidable excesses of the conscious, subjective, mind) guide your journey through *The Seventh Year.*

So, in all humility, embracing the same *Seussian* style of poetry, here is a sampling of my impressions, as both a participant and an observer. They are offered as a second eye to add to your own, in the hope that if so received, with no real judgement (explicit or implied), the reader may find a new perspective, a fresher outlook, and begin to see the doors to the future they did not know were there.

"As far as we can discern, the sole purpose of human existence is to kindle a light in the darkness of mere being"

C.G. Jung

A moral, even ethical concept. But from Jung's pen, it has an even deeper meaning. Good and Evil exist. As we emerged from the swamp, so are our first inclinations. But, once we learned to lift our eyes and look at the sky, greater thoughts arrived. Psychologically speaking, life without purpose cannot lead to psychological health

THE POEMS

PERSPECTIVE

"It all depends on how we look at things and not how they are in themselves"

C.G. Jung

WHAT I FOUND

July 2017

I've always looked to the sky

Never really knowing why

The road always led to some place

So I followed faithfully its trace

At times when things look dark

And the road was no longer bore any mark

Just keep looking ahead and the fog would lift

Waiting in some unexpected, a gift

Life can be generous if you believe

It is never her purpose to deceive

Her gifts are those of her choice

And they may not always make you rejoice

They can come wrapped in strange coverings

And often don't feel like "mothering"

But if her goal is to keep us awake

And not just for our own sake

A challenge may lie hidden inside

Often one from which we'd rather hide

Ugh! Another hill to climb

After the last one I'd wanted to resign

Haven't I earned a reprieve?

Deep down I know she will never deceive

With that in mind I've pushed forward

Up the hill towards the light, even if seemingly untoward

And now that I've reached the top of the hill

Tired, but believing to be wiser still

II look out on the vast valley ahead

Wondering is this where I am to make my bed?

But then it hits me like a brick

Has life played on me yet another trick?

Though I can see for miles this space vast and rich

There is indeed one significant hitch

Granted no with clarity of eye and of mind

Has it led me to where myself I now find?

But there is no treasure waiting for me to reveal

No epiphany, no magic, no jewels to steal

What has been waiting for me all this way

Is yet another journey, though my past weighs lighter today

To live is to honor Life, her purpose being

Not some final solution, all seeing

For if Life carries well its name

Nowadays we view her as passive, even lame

Her reality is there for all to know

It is to be born, to live, and to grow

Messy, chaotic, cruel and kind

Something to which we pay little mind

So having climbed the hill and the source of the light

All this time I was blinded, it was so bright

What awaits me, my reward, my illumination

Is more an intermediate solution

I've been given a blank new page

What I write on it will reflect my age

This is a new moment of my time here

Where I can live with more peace and less fear

No one owns me, I have no master

Except my desire to always move faster

Perhaps that too will slow down

After all why run all over town?

When what I seek is most likely near

What I have to do is clear

Remain engaged in the life that surrounds me

Find some way to share what has set me free

Continue my pursuit, my way

And greet with surprise each new day.

67

April 2017

Sixty Seven

Hell or Heaven

How it begins

Collecting on my sins

Some of the news was indeed good

At least that's how it looked from where I stood

Some was indeed less so

An emptiness appeared, one that I know

Life in balance, the eternal mix

Whatever I do, I find no fix

I am free, I now own my life

The chord was cut by clarity's knife

Doubts don't haunt me, I chose my way

Aware of each step's meaning, day by day

No map exists, no path is certain

Traps avoided, there is no curtain

Is that enough to be thankful for?

At least I'm still walking, searching for the door

It's strange to have known some degree of control

My road has brought me far towards being whole

Yet this road is different for each and everyone

Is there a moon for every sun?

For often I feel I've gotten ahead of the crowd

Have I gone too far, further than allowed?

My words intended to give strength and heal

More often frighten those so many, afraid to feel

Mind and heart, together a powerful force

My journey took me far afield, including a divorce

Never intended, married for life

Tricked by a deeply troubled wife

Others saw when I was blind

I found a purpose, a reason to be kind

It's a theme that's run through my time

Each endeavor started off well, seemingly fine

But as closer we got to crossing together that border

Things started misfiring, a sense of disorder

My eyes were fixed on the horizon, the unknown to meet

The road, smooth or broken, felt sure under my feet

I spoke words of encouragement, gazing to reassure

I felt the sun on my face, as we drew closer to the cure

I turned to smile, we were almost there

But no one was beside me, I was left alone to care

About the reasons why I do what I do

The one beside me had abandoned me, the one I thought I knew

After so many years of nourishing my hope

A knowing innocence helped me to cope

But now as I enter the dusk of my time

I seek no one to blame, nor do I whine

I've left that behind, knowing no one waits for me

At least insofar as I am able to see

Some say don't try to force things to come about

Continue down your path quietly, no need to shout

But time grows short, though not in a hurry

Can one turn clarity back into blurry?

One thing is for certain, a new door I must find

One that will lead me to a land where people care and are kind

Then I wonder, does that door truly exist?

Or was it a dream I saw in a mist?--

Did I miss some opportunity, timing can be all?

Was it the great adventure I wanted, or something small?

Never one for doubts, they lead nowhere worthwhile

What I am certain of, however, is our species has once again become vile

Writing is what I have now, Jung said to look within

Though what I am longing for has nothing of some sin

To care, eyes open, with no strings attached

Except those each shares, perfectly matched

Not in some superficial way, no style nor type

Both seeing life's light, no artifice nor hype

I've striven for some pure form, perhaps have I indeed gotten too far ahead

But once tasted such emotion, most others are bland, tasteless, even dead.

I end this poem, though its message has easily come

I'm still in the same place, my search must continue for I am not yet done.

WHAT'S REALLY IN THE WAY

"People will do anything, no matter how absurd, to avoid facing their own souls."

A NEW DOOR

April 2017

What do you do

When each avenue

Be they those less taken

Or by none forsaken

Advice abounds

Conventional wisdom resounds

In books, on tv, it makes the rounds

Though I listen carefully, I find their arguments offer no convincing grounds

Skeptical, perhaps, not easy to convince

My thoughts run deep and don't easily rinse

Listen, I do, solutions always come from left field

In the past that's how I have often healed.

But for the many, in fact, if that which they seek

Is just a small stretch, requiring but a tweek

Can hail success or write a book

Some minor effort is all it took

But if change were so simple, have we really taken a good look?

Just go to the library, Google, or buy some book

Follow the program, take a course, don't really question anything at all

Just don't look back to check if things improved, or did you drop once again the ball.

Ah, the motions one can fake

If change was sought for another's sake

If you were happy – sort of – with the way things were

Some superficial movements can another's vision blur

For me, though, my ambitions have too large grown

Along with what I have sought to discover, learn, and known

To satisfy the vision which defines the need

There's no place for facility, ease or greed.

For I've studied this question for so many years

Never did I let my inquiry be hindered by fears

I'd learned early on they are of two kinds

One useful, the other only reminds

Voices from the past, demons in fact

They exist not to counsel but to prevent us to act

Conservative to the extreme, when victims they were

For in the beginning, their purpose was not to deter

We see ourselves, of necessity, through others eyes

Ignoring their motives, desires and lies

So we prune ourselves, like some seedlings growing under a hood

Becoming more bonsais than pines, oaks or redwoods

But what if the road had been free, one's hero had been found?

And yet at some stage, it appears the boat had run aground

Applying every counsel, one's own and those of another

Yet each door seems to lead to no answer or solution other

Conclusion number one, what am I doing wrong

Time to change the music, find a new song

Here again, two thoughts come to mind

How does one know to live differently, that newness to find?

For I know what I know, not what I ignore

Obviously, that's why I can't find the right door

Has my curiosity run dry, have I become blind?

Is my head too full, clouding my mind?

Do I live in a place and time not made for me?

I live my life alone with myself in relative harmony

But those around me see things a different way

And when I speak, many are deranged by what – though not how –
I say

If that's the answer, an option starts to emerge

Move from this place, look inward for some guiding urge

But I've moved too often in my life, I'm tired of that

It's the opposite of what I want, a place to stay and hang my hat

I've built and rebuilt many times with relative ease

I have no problem meeting others, I'm easy to please

At least at a level social with no strain

I'm told of my qualities, my humor, my looks, my brain

But in this land of the quick fix

Serious questions rarely enter the mix

Where all problems should be solved with a pill

Who really wants to hear why this direction our spirits will kill?

"You think too much, over-analyze

Where's today's payback, I want my prize."

So there you go, my life's plan in shorthand

It seems I've reached a temporary dead end – and there taken my current stand

As has often happened in the years gone by

I see things in a different way, so I must try

Not to prove I am right, for I know other perspectives exist

I know more I can learn, not my first desire - to resist

Out of place, out of time, somehow in this land I am stuck

I can't blame or change the world, or pass the buck

So I write to think, hoping a new door to discover

And in so doing, a fresh future to recover.

There are days when hope start to run thin

To give up would be, in my view, the only sin

So rise and shine with the sun in the sky

And smile at Life, and ask her why.

THE PRICE OF WISDOM

"Mistakes are, after all, the foundations of truth, and if a man does not know what a thing is, it is at least an increase in knowledge if he knows what it is not."

C.G. Jung

A RIDDLE

May 2017

Here's a riddle, something not just for you

It's been around forever, though its numbers grew

I'd say more or less in the past 50 years

It's nature has changed with the growth of fears

The system, more competitive, yet in a different way

Has blunted the need to be truthful in all that we say

It's infected our culture through some fault of our own

Now there's a clue for you, has its cover just been blown?

If not, let's continue, quite the contrary in fact

That last statement plays its part in every infected act

At first we knew just what we did

It came easily when we were still a kid

When caught our thoughts turned instantly

Quick. Run and Flee. At worst come up with an implausible story

Point a finger at someone other

It works well with a sister or brother

What's perhaps less natural is our expectation

That as we grow older, we can find some salvation

In seeing things clearly, including other points of view

That's supposed to inform us all – now that's new

And with the years, this vision would grow wider and deep

Making it easier to learn and the acquired wisdom to keep

Is this really so – has it come to pass?

Have we all moved to the head of the class?

Now there you have quite a numbers of clues

Has the answer grown clearer, have I been a good muse?

If not ready yet, to venture a guess

Here's another – look around you – do you see the mess?

No- not yet? Then lets resume our course

At times awareness comes only from force

Does it derive from our long lost past?

It might have saved our skins if we couldn't run fast

There was a cost, even back then

Before things were written down with paper and pen

Proof then came into being, sort of a trap

We had to up the game to avoid the flap

Though nowadays, it's cost – though less – is seen as more

Even when predictable, when we know what's in store

Somehow we've evolved, if that's the right term

However we've let certain things grow lax, less firm

Any closer?   Has this become an annoying game?

Shall I pick up the pace or stay the same?

Another push then, to move us along

The melody may change, but not the song

When I left this land, we spoke in words more clear

When some vague threat was not ever-present, when there was less fear

A mistake, a falsehood, a wrong, a crime

Of course we knew to whom it belonged – It was theirs, not mine

Try though they may to not get caught

If successful, their freedom they bought

But never in doubt, there was a sense of guilt

No houses on lies of this nature were built

But somehow the more we have, the more fear of loss has
grown

And with it this ancient reflex its seed has sown

Avidity brings with it many a fault

There's just so much one can hide in a vault

This hunger without reason or limit or goal

Has stolen stealthily our culture's soul

For no longer do we seem to care about right and wrong

It's now " how much" and not "what's" the theme of the song

Ready for the answer? At least what I think

In every field, nothing escapes its stink

When wrong we do – intentional or not

What should we do to escape the plot?

That which would infect our very soul

Fragmenting our consciousness – not making it whole

To me it seems when in the wrong we've been found

It's normal to feel something, but are we really hell bound?

Or do we not learn most from where we go astray?

Is that not also the point of the games we play?

It's the consequences which change, but the message is the same

Acceptance of our errors and their sanctions – even if not tame

Is it really so dated to think that the harsher the fine

The more I might just make the lesson mine

So I will remember a choice along my road should I meet

How will I see it – will I flee or rush out to greet?

As if some old friend, forgetting the past

Is that not how old patterns our futures are cast?

Enough – I agree – this has gone on longer than I thought

But if I've made some headway – an insight's been bought

The answer is clear, have you divined its name?

It's what we do when we can – we pass along to another the blame

So next time you feel a twinge, something not quite right

Look in the mirror – be it day or night

Who is responsible – the truth is a gift not a curse?

And tell yourself truthfully which is worse

If I alone caused this wrong

If it's the consequence of a lifelong song

If it is something I've always chosen not to see?

How will I ever learn from it to be free?

A VOICE

December 2014

Here is a tale of caution, no longer told

Of a treasure meant not to be bought, traded or sold

A journey, a path, a formula to turn lead into gold

Yet like most great endeavors requiring courage, reserved for only the bold

We start knowing little of why we are here

Life beats us up, too often its first lesson is to fear

The essence of who we might otherwise come to be

Parts of which are chased into a darkness that we can no longer see

The role that was to be theirs as we make our way

A chorus of voices condemning them we heard one day

Silenced, as if evil demons, to be banished from our core

To be heard from no longer, not any more

Who were they to be reviled to such a degree

Were they evil or misunderstood so others could not see

That they were but small, not yet fully formed

If left to grow up, would they not have reformed?

So denied a place that was rightfully theirs

Banished to a dark place where no one cares

To live out their lives, for alive they were

These were pieces of ourselves, not some mangy curr

But to be good requires great sacrifice

Too often we neuter our children telling them to be nice

You can see them around, for quickly they learn

Two faced or rebellious, each taking its turn

Now children, of course, arrive in the world unprepared for what
waits

Hard wired baloney, certain demons exist and are there at the gates

Ready to pounce, for we come from a wild and dangerous place

And to live together, we must tame our race

Now there is a word one things of with beasts

Broken their spirits so our needs they meet

But tame is a gentler word, where wild can rest

Danger, once removed, they can show their best

Included in this gentler side are talents the wait

When brought together the two change their fate

Wholeness comes from the meeting of the two

Creating a third, entirely new

So the point of this rather convoluted rhyme

Which is taking me a great deal more of my time

If that when faced with a child or a beast

What you really want is to add some yeast?

To create a reaction that would not otherwise be there

Where what does not fit is not kicked down the stair

It can learn – a word I prefer over train

Why? Because all creatures have a brain

Though there are times when I watch peope with their pets

With hand signals, whistles, gadgets and the rest

Believing the dog instinctively will obey a simple click

Magic – the dog came preprogrammed by magic

They do the same with their children, though the currency may change

Why are so many parents so clueless?   it's really so strange

For they were children once, don't they recall

Or is everything imprinted so they just repeat it all

To know what to do starts with knowing oneself

To recognize whose pulling the strings from inside – demon or elf

And to have a serious talk with those voices inside

Bring them out in the open, don't make them hide

For that's the problem, imagine how it might feel

If you were told you were bad, hurt, and not allowed to heal

Would you not grow angry, resentful and mean?

If you were forced to live in the darkness, never to be seen

So make peace with yourself, as best you can

Know what's going on inside when your child you can't stand

Talk to that thing that has been punished long enough

Show them a little love and things will grow less tough

No longer the need to rule our lives and make us obey

But to bring their perspective into consciousness, so they can have their say

Like some diamond whose facets reflects life's different sides

Putting together these visions into one, the greater truth to abide

Thus could we walk into a future, more sure of our road

Finding the home for our hearts on this earthly abode

Not living some vague promise of a better place after we die

Where from underground I doubt even blessed souls can see the sky

Though incomplete perhaps, never truly whole

Each step thus taken, we approach ever closer the goal

Mistakes to be made, from them we learn the most

Revealing our blind arrogance: advance, don't just coast

Each step intended, revealing some necessary truth and sign

Thought the roads are always curved, never a straight line?

On our way, what are we to find?

How will we recognize that which truly nourishes our mind?

Is there an answer, simple and clear

One we can embrace a formula, and hold it near

A method, a recipe, a map to guide us through our fear

If such existed, its value would be greater than dear

No, step by step we move onto unknown ground

Never sure of what awaits, what will be found

But the arms we develop, the battles we win or lose

Contain something precious if we listen; how to better choose

To see where we've been, what we've done, what we truly desire

The deceit of fantasy burned away by life's fire

Of a hunger for life, to taste the many flavors at hand

To learn what we like, our direction, to take a stand

To define a meaning, a purpose, and find a path ahead

Not seeking simple pleasures too often repeated; be curious; alive, not dead

Though different we are, how we see the world, ourselves and others

Be they lovers, parents, children, sisters or brothers

What gives value, whatever the means

What defines what counts from what's worth beans

Resides in the heart, our emotions, our ability to care

Without it we wander aimlessly, neither here nor there

Yet how do we learn to look deep inside?

To places we're told to ignore, in favor of wealth and pride

Parents are there to teach us true

To learn there are reasons the sea is green and the sky is blue

Too busy, however, pursuing things that don't really count

Pile up the money and possessions, no matter the amount

Lost they are, their time misspent

Never owning their lives, living short term, they only rent'

Until it's too late, and the time is past

Learned nothing of value, what they built won't last

Houses, cars, iphones, even kids

No sense of what's important, mistaken bids

Where the cards fall, or the roulette ball drops

The fields yielded nothing useful but weeds and dying crop

So here is the warning, a cautionary tale

Have I got your attention, have I made the sale?

Are you ready to open your mind and find the north star

The one always visible from near or far

The one that is constant, from which to plot one's course

And to see appear our mount out of nowhere, the noble horse

The one rooted in nature, that which binds us all

Who will carry us forward and not allow us to fall

So approach it with care, intention and love

Climb up on its back, join together like hand in glove

And onward you go, beginning your quest

Like someone who belongs, and not just a guest

Take possession of your means, exploring desires

Some extinguish quickly, others burn like raging fires

Each one is meant to consume what we cared about before

And when the fire has gone out, what should remain is a new door

A challenge, some fear, curiosity and strength

The come unknown, we must go the length

Of this part of the road, until a new fork appears

Then consider where it leads with neither tears nor fears

They deform perception and fool our minds

Convince us that worthless would be these new finds

Filter away the glimmer of specks of gold

Telling us better not to strive, but give in, grow tired and old

Too many resign, blaming always something outside themselves

Magical thinking, it's not me, it's those damned elves

Hard wired, sick, old baggage – always something else to blame

Look outside, not in, that's the name of the game

In so doing what's happened, have I won or lost

Is there a prize, some money, a trip or just a cost

Only that which is ours is what we control

To believe that we have no say when the dice we roll

Seen that way, all that's left is the toll

Why pay it if prevents us from becoming whole?

If such is you view, you play the wrong game

Life gives us at least half the equation, but sadly no name

Do we try or simply embrace the randomness through resignation?

It seems such is the case in this "exceptional" nation

It is what it is – a favored refrain

To speak thus suggests we have neiter heart, nor soul, nor brain

What's left in its place is emptiness and pain

Stuck in place, it's already left the station, the train.

Enough of these warnings, dire and dark

I came to light a fire not extinguish the spark

So let the tale begin, in three phases it's told

Uncertain of how well I will tell it I must be bold

The message is clear, the path ahead most clear

In reading what comes, open you heart and put aside your fear

Let the story unfold, in new ways try and hear

And if you can, bring it into your heart, hold it near

Three souls, an evolution, connected in discernible ways

How the story develops may take years, months or days

Depending on the turns one takes

Determines how the batter bakes

A choice is present, for some an unpleasant fact

They prefer no ownership, guided by the past, they just act

But those who see an opening, a door waiting to be crossed

There's so much more to be won than could ever be lost

Does the pot of gold await us all

Applying the recipe, will we never fall?

Imperfect is life, its processes too

What doesn't work out we accept – there's no one to sue

And at the end of the day, of each day, whether dark or clear

If we open our hearts and have no fear

If we know in some sincere way, even in part, the direction we take

Another brick is added to this house that we make

Will it be finished at the end of our time?

Will others admire it and see it as mine?

Matters little, I've come as far as I could

Will my house last, is it made of bricks or wood?

Once again, in our difference, the aspect may change

Our garden may bloom with the seasons, this too we can rearrange

But the fundamental fact, the one that endures

The one that attracts likeminded others, that lures

Is this is our way, part fate, luck and choice

Who can know for we've played our cards; we've had a voice.

A WEDDING

Not forgetting though not yet there

Perhaps really not that fair

The day has finally come

When two together will make one

When the difference in years start to blend

A new message will it have to send

Youth takes its leave

It has a new life to weave

Defined by your choices

Forged by two separate voices

Each step a new block

Placed with thoughtful care, like some eternal rock

Serious now, for what you build

Will by what you do live or be killed

Not by outside interfering forces

Running random like wild horses

But by your will to make it work

Speak the fears and doubts that in shadows lurk

Bumps in the road, resentment and more

Along with progress, that's what's in store

Keep your eyes on the road

Soar above, don't hop around like some toad

See you goal, eyes fixed on the prize

That's to be the measure of your future lives.

So feel my presence, my spirit, my soul

Each separate, yet together, become whole

Learn from old mistakes gone by

Eyes not on the ground but on the sky

And as the road narrows as it nears its end

Look back, and to your own children this same message you will send.

Life's road is meant to live

Have faith and courage, gain less from take, more from give

Each in the other's corner

Always to cheer, never a mourner

Fill your lives with joy

Have children – a girl, a boy

And know your life knows no end

Whatever turn the road may take, whatever the bend

You will live in them, in this tree of life

Each branch bending, in love or strife

The shape it takes, that's who you are

With all my love, may it take you far.

ALL MY LIFE

All my life it seems I've searched for someone

Who, perhaps like me, was not meant – I thought - to live as one

There have been moments when I thought it   might be

If I am here, why not a few more –maybe   even two or three

When through whatever means the universe makes things right

I would sleep arms entwined, safe in the   night

The feeling comes, intense, so real

I place my critical sense aside to mostly feel

Not like those so loathe to trust

I have no choice in the matter – I must

Belief has always come easily to me

Confident in my heart, it has always been   free

Why hold back when wholeness beckons?

Life is short, why waste minutes or even   seconds?

Waiting for the sign that it was but an illusion

Or to ask oneself once its gone – was it all some delusion?

My heart exists but to care

Perhaps that's why it's so ready to dare

It sees a truth and knows a fake

It sees a truth and knows a fake

Whether I'm dreaming or wide awake

But what I've learned is that the truth I find

Does it exist only in my mind?

What's the reason it fails to last or prove true?

Why did it wither rather than grew?

That part of me which seems to call out

Is there something that makes me silently shout?

Attracting strangers in need of care

The connection is made, even they seem to dare

But the connection comes from one lonely part of them

Unlike flowers, it's but a leaf without the stem

It goes not down to the very root

Nor up to and including the fruit

Yet this leaf, this piece is in such need

What attracts them to me in the end is less care and more greed

For a time the hunger drives them to open their   hearts

And the roles they play differ from their usual parts

I live the dream, they dream the real

Fleeting for them is this ability to feel

But when the dream ends for them

When the leaf is sated and back home to its stem

A chill, a distance begins to take hold

And I can feel their hearts grow cold

While mine, as open as it ever was

Wants only to do what naturally it does

A pain stabs me deep in my core

Experience has taught me what's in store

The words of love, of loyalty evaporate

As they return to their normal state

While I torment myself with questions why

I burn inside while the others sigh

Until the inevitable end

Silence intrudes, but does not mend

Only time, and reason, make sense of it in part

I pick myself up, ready again to start

Wiser for sure, but no less unsatisfied

Why am I thus, I never lied?

Is sincerity a cross so hard to bear?

Why is it so frightening for others to care?

Have we always been a race of chameleons?

Depending on the circumstance to be whores or nuns

To fool unknowingly yet with such skill

To nourish a hungry heart just until

Before it can feel safe and secure

And finally know an enduring cure

I seem to heal after each time

My heart, though given, remains mine

And hope, for some reason, refusing to learnLike the sun, comes up daily, ready to burn

This makes me cheerful, never short of a smile

I walk alone each and every mile

Even my compagnons, canine though they be

Are taken too soon, with such brutality

Is life like that, the older we get?

Losing more often, though always placing the same bet?

Clinging to youth's illusions with promises led

Were they all lies that we were fed?

Alone, they say, we come into this world

Alone, at the end, into who knows what we are hurled

Hoping at least that with those we've lost to reunite

If we've lived a good life, and fought the good fight

I find these musings reserved to but a few

Are they meant to discourage or to renew?

Such insight, the fruit of a privileged time

Exists not for most others, and they seem to do just fine

Bathed in unconscioiusness, these matters ignored

At worst they don't suffer, at best they are just bored.

There are days when these thoughts burden my heart

No cheerfulness carries me, I feel separate, apart

Just the ordinariness of life deadens my soul

And oddly enough, I resume my place – alone, yet whole

ANYBODY

May 2017

When in my search, no one do I find

A shift occurs in my mind

The stars which emanate from my heart

Their constellation's clarity seems to fall apart

The pieces which began as a coherent whole

Split into disparate pieces, each with its separate role

One goes primal, all lust and thirst

To take what it wants, only it exists, its needs come first

The object, no longer a person, is there for one reason

To suit my mood, my hunger, my season

No significance in my acts, however violent or tame

It's forgotten as soon as it's over, the whole thing lame

For my choice is driven by bits and pieces

It's all about now, divergent needs and their singular releases

Pleasure is to be mine alone, and for a time that's brief

Emptiness returns, and I see what was - nothing was true

No structure, no rules, no purpose, no goal

Directing my actions as such risks a terrible toll

To continue thusly would dissolve that which holds the parts
together

The thing that will see me through any rough weather

For if anybody will suffice for a moment's pleasure

Should I someday find it, what will remain of the treasure?

The chest in this fashion can be emptied if care is not taken

If anybody will do, myself I will have forsaken.

FORTY YEARS

January 23, 2014

As your fortieth draws near

Thoughts of you, on occasion, appear

The fours seem to play a role in time measured

You put under lock and key, those lost or treasured

The father you cast aside in your turn

Was reprieved after fours years to maybe learn

What he had done and at what cost

What he wagered and what he lost

And now, fours years will have soon come and gone

Each on our own, we've carried on

I wonder at times, if the wounds did heal

Have hearts frozen over or can they still feel?

Were seeds that were planted, have they grown?

Has what was felt become understood and known?

For my part, I have continued my search for another you

Recalling those turbulent days when the sky was blue

I've sampled so much, at times thinking I'd found

A new safe haven, a heart, some solid ground

But in this land where roots shallow remain

Where deep emotion is feared, less a blessing, more a stain

Where time is measured in segments short

Where love we more often prefer to abort

At times lost, alone, the future obscured by a cloudy sky

Resilient I remain, always wondering why

I see clearly when others flea

How will it end, what will be?

Answers provide a moments peace

But there is no final release

The tension returns, born of shifting sands

We run to keep up, then watch it fall through our hands

Movement can't be stopped, things evolve

We all need something constant around which to revolve

Without it, where do we look?

There may be a pole, a line, but no hook

So cling to whatever seems surest even if broken

Regardless the truth, even if spoken

What's missing, why in fact, this buoy we need?

Is it just selfishness, insecurity or greed?

Do these questions now emerge in your fortieth year?

Will you face them with courage or fear?

And now that four years have passed, time well spent?

Are you ready to buy or do you still rent?

The prison, Stockholm Syndrome, co-dependent, alone

Has anything changed, in voice, message or tone?

One father recovered, though no will exists to resolve

Another found, provided safety perhaps, but together can you evolve?

A third – me – offered more, but you weren't ready

Too fragile still, your heart could not be steady

But now half your life, a landmark time

Arbitrary perhaps, but new insights awaken, a sign

That which guided you in the past

That which you thought immutable, in stone cast

Are called into question, answers no longer so sure

A chance, a turning point, a beginning, a cure?

The greys emerge from the black and white

Textured emotions fill the night

What will you do with this new day?

Will your heart speak again and what will it say?

Mine, as you know, to live must talk

I want to run, not content to walk

Perhaps you've come to see your time here has an end

Life is short, that's the message your fortieth will send

So what will you do – fight against time?

On whose side this time will you align?

And I wonder, if I saw you again, how it would feel?

How did the wounds heal – with a permanent seal?

All I know is that in my center you live, the essence of me

When I start to believe another you there cannot be

Emotions arise and discover new things to say

I see the sun rising to warm a new day

AYE – EYE

May 2017

Three year ago it all began

A hot day playing tennis of which I am a fan

A challenging partner, I raise my game

Interestingly, we shared the same first name

When suddenly, with no warning or sign

A red veil crossed my eye, though I felt fine

And so it started, this journey through time

Yet another reason why I've turned to rhyme

I have taken my lumps over the years

And for some reason, never abandoned myself to fears

Somehow confident that bad endings were for others than me

A youthful thought preserved, a hole in my maturity?

But it served me well each time fate knocked me down

Like the phoenix I rose, wearing a smile instead of a frown

Not some foolish child or optimist

It seemed to come naturally, if you get my gist

And in general, I can say

The sun came up on a brand new day

But this time – with others involved – things have taken another turn

And as is often the case, some new lesson I try to learn4

First metaphorically, what could this mean?

Monocular vision – I wasn't keen

So trust in the doctors, so confident

Who knew? Five failed surgeries – how was that meant?

Two more in succession – though less rapid this time

And after each one, I thought I'd be fine

But lo and behold, how easy these doctors turn

Their primary focus, their real concern

Was not me, for they work at an infernal pace

And who was I but just some other case

A technical challenge at best – feigning mild sympathy

Then dismissing me again, their words some meaningless cacophony

And we parted, new challenges of which I'd never been warned

And vague options unexplained, with worry I left, heavily adorned

So taking a few moments to digest my hurt

Then back in the drivers seat, vigilant and alert

I did my research, understanding came

And I started to realize the rules of this new game

Questions I ask, difficult for sure

Met with disdain – they found them hard to endure

Too bad I trusted too often in the past

I wanted back what should never been taken, and fast

These doctors close ranks quicker than any military force

Finding a malpractice lawyer more difficult than for divorce

No one cared that something precious had been taken

By each doctor I found myself first patronized, then forsaken

I went overseas, believing there money counted for less

To find someone perhaps to fix this mess

At first things looked promising – a clear indication was spoken

Heroic the solution for an eye so broken

Messages exchanged, engagements sought

When all of a sudden, it all came to naught

For this doctor so Swiss, disappeared into the night

I think humbled by the task at hand, so he took flight

Finally I've found someone willing to engage

That brought some solace and calmed my inner rage

So now it's clearer, at this point in my quest

There are few options, but none are the best

My eye looks gone, though it clings still to sight

And I retain the strength to continue the fight

But every time after the last consultation

I hit bottom once again, hurt and filled with frustration

For this should never have happened, fate chose to take

An eye – why – of this no sense can I make

How to explain this wound to my core?

With the practicalities I can deal, whatever's in store

Unless, of course, Life decides to take the other as well

And then I will have to live in a sightless hell

But we're not there yet, holding on to my trust

If I don't, who knows what, so therefore I must

What Life has taken at this point in time

Remaining hopeful, with that optimism of mine

I know now what to expect, so I must be fine

But something was lost as I consider surgeries eight and nine

Trust is a thing essential to us all

Hope, it's partner, responds when hearing the call

But just so often can the message mislead

If it happens too often, our souls start to bleed.

So doctors wherever you are

Remember the true guiding star

To heal is a gift, an honor, a prayer

To your patients, be kind, honest and fear not to care.

BELIEVE

February 24, 2015

From out of nowhere the darkest of clouds appeared

Like some fire raging across the land, my heart it seared

Whispers of loss these past weeks spoke and I feared

Sensing its approach as it neared

Take notice but little, not wanting to believe

Too soon again to start to grieve

Though she'd been with me for awhile

A unique blend of innocence and guile

The thought of my flower's spring coming to an end

Science unable the insult to mend

So what was left for me to do

What arms do I have against a foe old, yet always new

Only those that are mine, they reside deep in my chest

These are the ones I know best

My first thought is to my own promises broken

Have my sins through her been spoken?

God is there to hear it all

It's when we need him the most that we issue the call

No words come in answer, rarely clear at all

Up to us to feel our faithl rise or fall

They aren't sharp, lethal or mean

They come from the other side, where shines a light clean

In their own way they battle against the encroaching fate

How or why they may work, will they come in time or be too late?

We cling to the hope the outcome to change

Until the last moment, fate to derange

Yet knowing we've lost, translated to pain

Hope is gone, only emptiness to remain.

What's Really Holding You Back

"Until you make the unconscious conscious it will direct your life"

C.G. Jung

BIRTHDAY 39

April 2013

The end of March is fast approaching

The time left to me to write is fast encroaching

I think of you often – as much for me as for you

Still not sure who is getting what they are due

I write for myself, stolen moments from the past

Refusing to abandon that which I wanted so much to last

Subjective these thoughts, the emotions endure

They bring solace but alas no final cure

I wonder still what use you make of my verse

Do they make you feel better, or do they make you feel worse

I hope for the former, for love wants only the best

But within this feeling resides a necessary test

One that will always challenge you in ways your abhor

For reasons I've spoken of often, no need to further explore

A conundrum, a dilemma, a knot with no end

And yet these messages I continue to send

Is it a gestation, a period of invisible growth?

For me or you or better yet, both?

A port of call, a safe haven, a home?

Safe from the waters and its surging foam

Was it a dream, a lie, a figment of mine?

I've looked deep within for some clarifying sign

But certainty of this type I do not own

It can't be defined by one person all alone

The answer requires, like some complex equation

A lengthy process of elucidation

No shortcuts, no steps skipped, no easy solution

Each operation depends on what came before for its final resolution

So where are we in this process, complex and long?

Am I alone to hear the melody which precedes the song?

I play my part as my heart guides my way

For a time I am silent until I have something to say

But keep this alive for purposes perhaps unclear

I won't let it yet die, so I keep you near

It gives me hope that love does exist

Even if its path holds many a twist

A symbol of what it feels like to care

Whoever said love was supposed to be fair?

So as your third decade draws to a close

As you look back on the pathways you chose

Have the seeds I've planted taken root?

Have you found nourishment from them like some precious fruit?

Has the baby inside you, the new you waiting to be born?

Is your hair still growing, or have you had it shorn?

Have you allowed yourself more clearly to see?

Have you found a way to become what you want to be?

So on this day of your 39 years

Are you still emprisoned by your fears?

That you cannot be who you are

Have you been able to see that far?

These things I send, my gifts to you

You are more special than you think......if you but knew...

BORN IN THE TIME OF GREED

December 2016

To be born in this time of greed

When to meet each and every need

Thoughts turn to things we can buy

With money, drugs, sex – get high

Yet no up can last, nor avoid its down

The short lived smile turns too soon to a frown

So the search goes on for something that will last

Yet no one seems to learn from the past

With each now possession – be it person or thing

Only furtive pleasures do they bring

With each deception the emptiness grows

Why is it no one knows?

Who can make me happy, who can make it last?

Why do I grow bored so very fast?

One doubles down, prowling for that thing

That will make one feel like a queen or a king

The succession continues, accelerates its pace

Are we living or just running a race?

Connection, chemistry, hot and fun

Either they can't be found, or they're gone on the run

Something is missing, there's nothing that seems real

Why is it these things don't make us feel?

It must be their fault, for I know I'm good

Or is it that I've not done all that I could?

That disturbing thought calls one into question

No one had prepared us for such a personal digression

Fragile is the one who ignores his mind

Growing frightened and shallow, selfish, unkind

Alone I stand, nothing touches my heart

In a crowd I may be, but I feel so apart

This is not me for I may belong in another time

I sense the sadness surrounding me, not only mine

The evil which makes us thus is the answer they cannot see

How does one find the path to be whole and free?

Is that even the goal, ask any friend or foe

They'll look at you as if they could not know

The question has been lost, like some treasure from an earlier time

Is all that's left for us to do is pine?

There is no process, no technique, no course

No shortcut, no riddle, no lecture – one cannot force

Into conscious what was never taught

These days our solution would be to have it bought

Like another possession, take it out of the box

Plug it in, secure its locks

Listen carefully, follow each phase

But nothing happens – should I be amazed?

Everything in life is destined to be understood

To begin the search, one must look carefully under the hood

And not just the pieces or the schematic provided

It's how it all comes together – not divided

Have we abandoned a deeper understanding?

When the life we engendered became too demanding

Unable to grasp this larger whole

We tossed in the towel, and damned be the toll

If what is bigger than us is just too hard to know

Retreat to the practical and make believe it's so

Dismiss w hat can't be broken into operational pieces

And look for the nuts and bolts that it greases

For what else but the concrete, the material side

Some fundamental security would it provide

Money the measure, pushing all else aside

The more I accumulate, the easier it becomes to hide

The comparison is a metaphor, for life now isn't that bad

We have so much more now than we've ever had

But in the process, in the race it's become

The important things have been lost to fun

Must life be only serious, with all that it brings?

Joys and tragedies, to common men and kings

Or if we recall there's more than only one side

If we remember that our truth lies inside

What we acquire of material things

Perhaps in the moment, makes our heart sing

But how long can it last, this ephemeral joy?

Devalued in a moment, it's little more than a toy

Then we begin to long for whatever is new

And if it's hard to find and reserved for the few

We'll look at what yesterday made our heart sing

Hell, it was only a bracelet or a ring

What lives outside, what we can physically acquire

Can be just as easily taken or lost in a fire

But the treasure that resides deep within

Can never be taken, only abandoned by sin

So if you're heart feels empty, with a sense of void

If no pleasure satisfies and you are readily annoyed

Ask yourself this – where do my true treasures originate?

Is my heart full or is empty my plate?

CHRISTOPHER

From the Chris/Hank Series

April 2017

A child conceived by a thoughtless two

Their motives selfish, cruel, unconcerned by what to do

Creating a life neither desired

An evil spell was thusly fired

Not designed to burn away elements impure

But to set a course that the child must endure

Looking now at this child and what he's become

A web of fears, lies, never loved – the tragic sum

Much talk of a hope for better days

Facsimile for a while pays

But slowly cornered, caught in his lies

From the safest haven he ever knew, he flies

Back to the mean streets, surviving at best

Unable to end it all, whatever the test

A chameleon, intuitive, still young enough to please

He must ply has wares, ever fearful of disease

No reason can reach him, though intelligence does not lack

He travels now lightly, his few things carried in the odd sack

How sad to see a life thusly spent

Was there ever a chance of another outcome that meant?

He could aspire to more, to one day be free

Of this cursed past that won't let him be

Too many lies have been told, too scared of the truth

More at home in the streets with other lost souls, uncouth

Trust is his mantra, once betrayed always the same

When asked if he himself is trustworthy, he changes the game

Skilled at deception, distraction, ill humor displayed

All designed to confuse as whatever new bonds formed grow frayed

Until, as must happen, the tricks cease to work

Retreat back to the jungle to live where his demons lurk

There more at home where the illusion can endure

That's the world he's always known, the one of which he's sure ow ironic that the one thing he does crave

Is beyond his reach, not knowing how to be brave

To live in a world so fluid and unkind

Surely must play tricks on even the most solid mind

For one never cared for, never love to be known

It weighs on his spirit like some enormous stone

From this flux, a fatal fantasy was spun

He's the center of some imagined conspiracy, he's the one

They track him in the streets, online and his phone

Though he's done nothing wrong for which he need atone

It's his way of feeling wanted, though pursued is not quite the same

He believes some higher up keeps tabs on him, though knows not his name

Whenever he starts to let someone get near

Alarms go off, driven by fear

From normal to paranoid, one can see the transformation occur

A wry evil smile takes hold, and emerges some wild cur

An animal alone, who lives only to fight

This angry beast wanders alone into the dark night

Looking for violence to vent his rage

More like a teenager than a man of his age

But a gentler soul resides deep within

One without defenses, so he relies on his second skin

Truly opposites they are, knowing each other well

This evil Hank holds him fast in his spell

For once abandoned, twice then three times

Who cares for promises – to him simple nursery rhymes

Daring anyone, he flaunts his fearless nature, a boast

Though no longer capable of wronging his host

The one person who showed him how others do live

How pleasure is taken less from taking and more to give

Tempting this dream, though out of his grasp

There is no holding him back, the friendly hand he cannot clasp

The hand that is tendered by one who sees the pain

Doing the right thing by this friend his only gain

Yet so many times salvation tried and failed

Forced to acknowledge now as his chances have paled.

The last one has come and gone, though both did try

For a brief time Christopher could look up and dream of a more benevolent sky

But the stone is too heavy, it's part of his life

There will be no rescue nor respite , no friend, nor wife

These agents who pursue him, for whom do they labor?

He only wants to know who they are – enemy or neighbor?

The mystery will endure, for he is blind

They are his inner demons, of the Hank kind

Even when I ask, why do they pursue him so

What is it about him that they must know?

No answer suffices, "annoying" he claims

And assigns them 00 numbers instead of names

Taking pictures for some file, imagined not real

The true enemy he fears most – that he might someday feel

Form an attachment, to trust, to have something of his own

It's too great a risk, forever his greatest unknown.

So gone now, for good I think, he's out of tricks

On to the next one for whatever fix

The wheels must spin endlessly, no time to pause, stop or think

Caught in this whirlpool he swims but can't seem to sink

To acknowledge the truth would exact too high a cost

For Hank is his soulmate, without him he'd be lost.

Whatever it is, this efidice, part of him thinks it's somehow
just fine

The logic isn't there, the fantasy predates that time

All he knows is the single, lonely word – mine.

So between Christopher and Hank, endlessly crossing the line

Unable to choose finally who he will be

Yet in spite of all he's learned, this truth he can't see

Alone he came into this world, unloved, undesired

One day, I think, of this race he'll grow tired

And on that day, he may just disappear

Devoured from within by anger, sadness, and most of all fear.

CHRYSALIS

April 2017

I used to know how to hope

Whatever the situation I could always cope

Projecting myself into a better time

Believing there was a place reserved that would be mine

And so it was for many years

I knew some joys and shed some tears

Yet in all, I think I lived with no great fear

Of a future where my place was clear

Yet today, just a few days past my birthday

Almost nothing seems to go my way

I've tried all I've known, olds solutions and new

But success continued to evade me – what to do?

Where does one go when nothing calls out to you?

When your options are exhausted and the new doors are few

When those you've loved or who you thought loved you

Are seen differently, strangers now that you once knew

A loneliness starts to materialize

Out of the mist before your eyes

Still too soon to identify or recognize

Dread and hope mix together, dissolving old ties

With no place to run, nor to hide

All one can do is one's time abide

And wait and hope and watch as the thing takes form

Disquieted, wondering, will this be some new norm

A way forward born of necessity

When the ways of the past offer no felicity

I think of the caterpillar, trapped in some husk

Not knowing why or when, dawn or dusk

What can it hear, what can it see?

"What is to become of me?"

Time may weigh heavy, ignoring the transformation

What will be the final destination?

If on the positive side, this phase sees the caterpillar reborn

Into another creature, deemed more beautiful, our world to adorn

But how does it reconcile who it was from who it's become?

Is there meant to be some continuity between the two and the one?

Does one remember or does one forget?

The past is gone, the future to beget

And what of the wisdom, so dearly paid

Does it stay the same or is it remade?

To serve its new host, with an existence all new

And what of its capabilities, all the different things it can do

Superficially it may seem a wondrous thing

To change from a peasant into a king

But this is to see things from the outside in

Is that not a mortal sin?

For what truly counts, what drives the change

Can only come from deep inside to so completely rearrange

This must be a fearful time for nothing's to be the same

One may sense a familiarity, but what is my new name?

What is mine to have or to claim?

Am I to be recognized or unknown with no fame?

And so it is, as this strange feeling slowly takes hold

My usual feelings of impetuous courage have gone cold

Thank God my routine remains intact

I can continue to live, to breathe, to act

As I've struggled these recent years, searching for what I thought I knew

Never did I suspect such a change as by the years flew

Knocking on the same doors, expecting a different result

Ignoring I was headed back to Nature's cult

Set aside this desire for progress, the need for some control

Life decides how long I must reside in this bowl

Where I have no longer much of a say

All I can do is to wait for my day.

The future is forming inside this womb

It may feel clautophobic like some tomb

But faith requires us to see the process to its end

And believe the fabric of life it will mend.

NORMALCY. THE GREAT ENEMY OF OUR FUTURE

"Show me a sane man and I will cure him for you"

C.G. Jung*"*

CONFUSION

May 2, 2012

Confusion, that state of mind

When things seem unsettled, unfamiliar, unkind

It's a place where too many stay too long

Like a chorus too oft repeated of some popular song

But what is confusion? A permanent home?

One ultimately designed to keep one alone?

When life offers a chance to find who one seeks

Why is attraction followed by confusion after only a few weeks?

The answer oft given is "it's complicated," I'm confused

Is it me or the other or both who are being abused?

Confusion reflects a choice, a chance

To embrace life fully, or sit out the dance

So many excuses we offer ourselves

As we watch life go by sitting on the shelves

Of our fears and our hopes – we get caught in between

Some days the lights are red, others they turn green

But it seems as time moves forward, the days go by

The noises of pleasure give way to reluctant sighs

What to do for both sides tend to merge?

Joy's song transforms into some inevitable dirge

Confusion is meant as a transitory state

How much should I eat? How do I feel about what's on my plate?

Am I hungry – of course – that is for sure

The first impulse provides the answer, simple and pure

But dare I believe, can I pull this off?

Is the table set for me or do I feed at some communal trough?

Thoughts and voices from the past grow with each passing day

The heart's yearnings are smothered, forbidden to have their say

With each decision put off, delayed or ignored

Confusion gains ground, and the mind grows bored

For why want something if it is to be denied?

And the reasons evoked, to myself I've lied

A vicious cycle of frustrated desire

The heart deflates like some punctured tire

If I do not stand and defend my needs

The past grows stronger, I get lost in the weeds

But is it by chance or an act of will?

It becomes easier with doubt my heart to fill

Not for me, but for others, or so it seems

Deluded in fantasy, they wander lost in their dreams

To believe what they say, only to recoil in the act

This is not some illusion, but a fateful fact

Embrace confusion, the faithless of heart

It provides a moments comfort these excuses but really serve to keep them apart

Imagining that to do nothing is the safer way

Silence these voices, why hear what they say?

Inaction results, passivity gains

It's not that bad these gnawing pains

What should be a temporary state

Our minds pierce the clouds so confusion can abate

But only if these detours and feints

Are seen for what they are, and what they ain't

So continue to believe in the tricks you deploy

Be wily, be expedient, with your own life be coy

Mistake your prison for a castle but know that it's your choice

When the truth you've silenced and shut down its voice

When you build a fortress of deceit and call it a castle

When lies calls and your answer is facile

The difference twixt the two so clear to see

One will emprison you, the other can set you free.

Cut the knot of confusion, some strings have neither beginning nor end

When confusion endures, appear inevitable holes in the fabric one cannot mend

CONTRARY

February 2015

Contrary is a land where there is no fun

Where the moon is mistaken for the sun

The clear lines which fix the cardinal directions

Are moving, unstable, shifting with no stable intersections

So how to set a course when the North Star moves

No one can stay the course with such shallow grooves

And what of the short term, those decisions to be made every day

The voices of advice seem to confuse as each will have its say

When all "knowledge" goes without critique

All opinion driven by personal pique

How do others know what to some appears like escape

Over and over in their minds, they seem to play the same tape

No new answers emerge with each repetition

Just more hesitation delaying a decision

Parameters, criterion, decision support

All are now arbitrary in judgements court

Some say do as Alexander did

Cut the Gordian knot when almost still a kid

But already therein were the seeds

Of a clear sighted mind ready for each required deed

Times have changed, no heroes speak

Our store of knowledge has sprung a leak

Facts are meaningless unless seen in their   interdependence

Each one subjectively selected to support my defence

The truth will escape me leaving only behind

A self-serving vision existing to support my mind

More is lost, reality impoverished

Minds can't prosper when undernourished

Not fed a diet of shorthanded junk

No leader, no hero, no wise man – a punk!

The mind, to fulfill its purpose overall

Must constantly move forward, without questions it can only stall

This innovation, acclaimed the cure to all economic woes

Serves mostly itself, on thoughtfulness, raining disqualifying blows

Deregulation, acquisitions, mergers as such

After the fact don't seem to accomplish that much

Change for change's sake is a fool's course

Blind faith that "new" by definition works only in the short term bourse

They've sold their message with bravado, repetition and most of all, stealth

Seeing change for its own sake, the source of most new riches

But the cost – has anyone given much thought to the road's new ditches

So here too, words mean only what I intend them to say

They are engineered to ensure my version will carry the day

Without rigor of meaning, of thought and word most of all

Meta-language gains legitimacy and ensures a preciptious fall

Listen to our discourse in the public or private domain

The abuse it's subjected to is little if not inane

Where is the nuance, the perspective, the synthesis, the right thought?

In this web of approximate, like bitcoin, no real substance is bought

No absolutes exist to anchor our reason

And thus have we committed the ultimate treason

Those who suffer most, for whom each decision is tough

Deeper they stray into the rough

Uncritically in the logical sense

Unknowlngly confusion becomes more dense

The more they indulge in what may look like thought

More convoluted the reasoning becomes, their conclusions come to naught

The roots of this malaise in childhood resides

When, as in each family, there were always two sides

One sought its version of structure, clarity and rules

The other saw such differences as a threat, the way of   fools

Both may not be wrong, or for that matter right.

What provides the most solid foundation should prevail in this fight

But primitive emotions and loyalties misplaced

With arsenic this brew from the outset is laced

To make a determination, to set that course

One must take a side and pick a horse

The choice is not about tribal loyalty or misplaced belief

Such leaps of faith fuel the fire and bring no relief

Some have no choice but to fight for their view

To do otherwise, plunges them into some swirling brew

Opposition, more than affirmation, sets the course new

In delay resides the power of the few

No progress can be built on the "no."

It's like sewing seeds in the desert where little can grow

And that which emerges is distorted and confused

Clearly the wrong approach is being used

The scene is set, they mount on life's stage

Little matter whatever their age

Lumps they take, fall they will

Bruised and battered – it's also part of the bill

But out of this turmoil, this cauldron, something is forged

Starts to emerge, take shape, as if from the rock   disgorged

A pretty picture of a future malignant

A country which believes more than knows is ignorant

When facts that are proven are cast aside

We'd all better start looking for a place to hide.

CONVERSATIONAL SEX

January 2017

Now let's talk about sex like an adult

Frank, open-minded and honest – after all, we're not in some cult

A group of people who claim an answer they've found

Who believe that sex can carry any weight built on solid ground

For if one listens closely to how people talk

One hears all sorts, only at the most obvious do they seem to balk

The words now used to express desire

Reflect more vile baseness than those meant inspire

Is sex not a joining, if from pure instinct we've grown?

Is it procreation and seeds thoughtlessly sown?

Have we forgotten how two people can heal

When the connection's purpose is more an emotion to feel

Listen to the banter, what the words reveal

To fuck, for example, a verb, often the result of some deal

It's something done to another, not shared in fact

One fucks, or is fucked, where's the joining in the act?

Body parts, that's what we've become

The bigger the better, be it breasts or a man's gun

Hot the adjective, the objective fun

And once it's over, "see you around," we're done

Try falling asleep in each other's arms

Savoring the peace with all its charms

But no, this closeness brought no intimacy or trust

Just a dose of fluids and momentarily satisfied lust

For that's what it seems, what happened to the rest?

As long as it's big, it will pass the test

Hot is a word so often used by the young

Like certain groups equate it with a question – " big tits," or "how hung?"

Others accept the premise no one partner can suffice

When the itch does strike, is it love or lice?

De we ever dream of the place sex might occupy?

Of all the answers offered – is there some truth to be found or another lie?

Some speak of hard wiring, others of drive

Vital sex is to stay healthy and alive

Really? That assumes it equates with other vital functions

Like breathing, and eating, and elimination – no compunctions

They must be satisfied, one of nature's golden rules

But if that were so, how did we become such slaves to it, such fools

Vows are taken, promises are made

How's this – polyamourous – partiers, let's just trade

Better than swingers, who seek anonymous fun

The poly's, more sincere, they don't jump the gun

They embrace continuity, until complications set in

Rationalizations intervene to justify the sin

Open relationships – today favored by many

The sex in their couple has run dry, there isn't any

So don't ask, don't tell, don't discuss – the lie is born

From anonymous encounter or ongoing liason – the family fabric is torn

No discussion is possible, that might rock the boat

What would one say? Just keep things afloat

Straight or gay, it seems no one knows anymore

What they do or why they do it – that question is such a bore?

More examples are there for any to see

Yet remains the question, why should this be?

If indeed we are a species of a higher mind

Should our drives not be of a likewise higher kind?

Has sex just become shorthand for any fascination?

Since it is considered the true test and foundation

Of any durable relation

So we must stink at it as shrinks its duration

I've pondered this from perspectives many

The scientific explanations don't offer real answers, not any

Nothing of use to help one understand

Why so many spend their lives lying, forced to live underhand

So let's back up, take a fresh look at the question

Is sex the equivalent of something greater than the endpoint of digestion?

It can take many forms, so we've reduced it to this

As long as the genitals are involved, no need for a kiss?

A kiss – that expression of affection – so intimate and dear

People recoil from it, most out of fear

For a kiss can suggest commitment and intimacy

Some prefer sailing on the oceans of sexual profligacy.

Hit and run.

Hot and fun.

When did this thing shrink so

And why are they so afraid honest answers to know?

For some, a kiss is Freud's oral phase

To satisfy a hunger, some genital malaise

Devour with something close to rage

Indeed, we have come of age.

For in truth, a kiss is intimate, a vulnerable state is required

"No way could I want that, I'm an outlaw whose gun is hired"

It shoots its way through any situation with nary a thought

"I got what I wanted, with no strings, a real bargain I caught"

But wait, if it's only the equivalent of a moment's pleasure

Where is the value, the meaning, the treasure?

And if over time, we've lost our way

Why do we do this, and for ourselves, what do we have to say?

Now there's the clue we've been looking for, a place to start

To have something to say, one must engage the heart

For this organ, though pump may it be

Is the seat of emotion, the eternal sea

From which we recognize what we value the most

Without it, landbound we are, stuck on the coast

Now having something to say, could it really be

Sex is a language, spoken by the body

It requires a connection, someone with whom to share

And being the body's language, soul and body to bare

Set aside the artifice, the insecurities, the mask

Vunerable and open, we learn to ask

To know me, and help me see into my heart

To recognize what is whole and what has been broken apart

To heal these wounds accumulated over the years

That have poisoned my mind with useless fears.

A give and take, perhaps similar but never the same

Uncensored, unafraid – spontaneous the first rule of the game

Next comes courage, to acknowledge one's own emotion

Not get stuck in some side road of co-dependency or false devotion

Sincerity can flow, feeding trust on the way

To travel on the road to intimacy, there is a toll to pay

Once the bonds of trust established, sincerity is known

Something new has finally grown

Like anything living, it requires care

If it is to survive and flourish, one must dare

To speak from one's heart, the truth unadorned

Through deception and artifice is love suborned

But if courage has taken hold and these hearts have grown bold

If spontaneity and curiosity have prospered as we have grown old

We will have found a source that can never run dry

All you must do is simply try.

Does this sound too easy, another quick fix?

Have I not taken something complex and made it simple, in the mix?

Do I pronounce some special words, as if by magic or tricks?

Have I built my house of hay, wood or bricks?

And to make it all work together, to make it last

To care for the other, when of necessity the passion has passed

The former, nature's canny invention, designed purely to attract

Was never intended to endure, through the final act

It's an act of will that must bridge every crater

If now together survives until later

Look back on yourself, what was sex for you?

Did you use words like hot, fun, amazing – but was it always new?

Like a conversation, if it's changing, never the same

If I abandon control, routine, repetition and invent a new game

If the partners truly think not of some fantasy but of each other

Not someone from the office, a cousin, a sister, a brother

The moment of truth, the joining takes place

And time can stop, it's no longer a race

Inside these parentheses, one wants only to take the time

To explore, to discover, to share – not alone – and make you mine

Not to possess, for to own is to ignore

And sex with an object quickly becomes a bore

The truth resides in something Juliet said

Since the first moment I heard it, it has never left my head

"The more I give, the more I have" to Romeo she spoke

As if in a dream from which she never awoke

To give is to look inside oneself, to find one's care

Embracing a heart that is full, courageous, one that can dare

To reach out of itself, to give and be received

There is no take for all value lies within; no longer deceived

Appearance, the screen on which fantasies lie

Can't match this source that will never run dry

If one can love, knowing no longer how to be alone

To stop and live in the moment, and simply be home

To see the wealth that is at hand

It's time to drop anchor, you will have finally reached land.

So after this lengthy journey, a shorthand at best

Can the question be answered? Can it pass the test?

Sex is the body speaking in a tongue of its own, unique

Somehow it's a language we have forgotten how to speak

For a touch is something real, it can stop time

Two bodies can become an inexhaustible mine

For the vein of gold runs very deep

And if found, the love it represents can be yours to keep.

Let it fill you with the richness that only you can provide

Stop the fucking, make love, lose the divide

Join with that person who somehow saw something in you

It's only if you reveal yourself can anything be really true.

THE DEATH OF EXPERTISE

June 2017

What is it about America that we have this need to know?

Is the hunger so great that we fear to go slow?

There is a buzz, an excitement, which we proclaim

To be our savior, our dvantage, even our aim

To out compete all others and win every race

Have we forgotten something essential as we increase the pace?

To learn something requires effort and time

To possess any subject – if that's the right term – and make it mine

What are the elements required, the process, the knowing?

We used to employ a different term than today – we used to call it growing

For we can accumulate bits of information – let's call them facts

In the quantified world, the more we have, the surer we can be when we act

Is it really just a matter of retrospective data and modeling projection?

To predict an outcome and point our nation in a designated direction

We've tried this on so many occasions, and we've been wrong

Does that mean we toss out the music and from scratch write a new song?

Or was the error just as complex as the case?

No one likes to be wrong, so we spin to save face

Without ever truly asking ourselves – where did I go astray?

I can't do that – if an mistake is admitted once, who would listen in the future to what I might have to say?

Even if wiser having gone back to the start

Who's got time when our focus is to be the most smart?

So there's another part of the erroneous equation

An imperative inherent in our self-inflation

I have been best before, so I must be again

Its America's birthright to always be a 10

Now stop for a moment – how realistic is that?

Look around you – been to a WalMart lately? Talk about fat!

Is the answer to conclude an error in our code?

That's starting the quest in the middle – a dark future forbode

So if we must be first, out of pride rather than need

What sin awaits – aside from greed?

To learn is a savant blend of facts and observation

Tempered over time with perspective and careful consideration

For to learn is an alchemy, impurities eliminated over a slow burn

With discussion, debate, doubt, and humility so necessary at each
and every turn

Out of the heated mixture, clarity emerges from the churn

That's what's involved when we take the time to truly learn

But another byproduct rises, the one we should always seek

For it will reveal not the whole truth but a hint of the future, a peak

Each answer reveals the next question, this be the real prize

But somehow we've forgotten this, for we fail to realize

That there is more we don't know that the sum of all we have
learned

That's the beauty of the mind, it's the vessel where all comes
together, on which fate has always turned

For the one who knows humility, all expert they be

Only they will have an open-mind, and above all, a healthy
curiosity

So here's a message to allour experts from the many different fields

Ask yourself how you've come by your learning, and what have
been its yields?

Is it more about recognition, money, status or fame?

Should you really carry the imprimatur of expert in name?

Wise is the one who knows how small is his space

How vast is the universe and how insignificant his place

How limited we are with our meager tools

Those swollen with conviction – beware the fools

Doubt is a healthy component of knowledge, essential to find

Without it, all we have is a brain. What happened to our mind?

So let's not mourn too long for expertise

If misunderstood, it's little more than a tease

Wisdom takes time, there's so much to consider

Quick answers are worthless, regardless the bidder

Like any object unique and refined

Can it be mass-produced or 3d printed, easy to find?

Would something not be missing, however precise the measure?

Too much is abandoned in the rush for treasure

A dinosaur I've often claimed to be

With views no longer holding much currency

But for the sum to be greater than all of its parts

We should include more unknowns in our savant charts

DREAMS HE NEVER HAD

From the Chris/Hank Series

June 2017

His dreams, those he buried deep

The ones his heart is supposed to keep

Has he abandoned them one by one?

No father to help build them with his son?

Another orphan in his place

Emptied of his own dreams, the blank face

A child's innocent smile broad and wide

Trying to win approval rather than is tears to hide

Frustrated, ignored time after time

Innocence gave way to mischief, too often crossing a line

Adults saw him as an annoyance at best

Only his father's mistress passed the test

Though his family was large it took someone from outside

Illicitly related to his father's mistress, In her arms he could hide

But this was to be but for a brief time

It remains, however, the only childhood memory that would shine

But you, I feel your loss, given away

With no dreams, no future – so heavy a price to pay

Only one at a time, each following the other

With no soul, no joy, only a loving brother

A family built at 15 from odds and ends

At least it was something, something real that mends

It lasted for awhile, a routine to create

Where caring had a home instead of hate

Why so shorlived, was it not meant to be?

Could no one the future see?

Not long after occurred a double tragedy

No friend, nor peace for him was ever meant to be

Best friend, brother, shot in the head, a settling of scores

Closed thusly on this brief moment were all windows and doors

No one wanted to know, none wanted to see

How these children lived abandoned, not free

The only friend he'd had lay dead in the street

Perhaps then too, his fate did he meet

Alone once again, the healing abrupty came to an end

I think all that was left was to run and defend

The conclusion had now become inescapable

To believe in hope again – now and forever, he became incapable

If that was indeed the case, what was he to do?

With nothing to lose, he took his cue

If the world was to be so cruel to him

He who'd committed no cardinal

If Life would strike him at his heart

This world, he want not any part

No resources of his own, drugs were easy to sell

The tough guy façade grew, and all seemed to go well

Experimentation, any means to send the pain away

Senses dulled, yet convinced there would never be a better day

There was another irony added to the mix

That a certain sunshine from within could not durably fix

A big smile shone through from his brave heart

Always there to take the underdog's part

To please, to find approval, something in which to believe

He would have to let go of this painful past and grieve

But like a candle burning from both ends

Fate sabotaged his chances, no way to make amends

These moments came to break solitude's pain

He could be generous ,with no need for praise or gain

But darkness was always close behind

Devouring the faint light lingering in his mind

No real salvation was ever to come

He'd held and lost hope, that's when the end was begun

The years came and went, somehow he survived

Running always from the law or the gangs, he bribed

A chance arrived one day for a legitimate life

Could he take the step and abandon the knife?

The danger he felt always at his heels

He would have to give it up if he were to find the wheels

To put them back so the train could finally move

Leave behind the rut and find a new groove

And for a time, he lived without strife

Beginning again to want a different life

Mean had decided this too was not meant to be

Unemployed, homeless in his years, six and twenty

For awhile, the odd job was found

Money in his pocket, could he be homeward bound?

Not some real one, with a family and all

That would be for him an order too tall

How much did he really need?

For his starved heart to feed

But nothing ever seemed to last

He raced through things, always going too fast

The rise, like the ultimate fall

Too soon, in slow motion, he was to lose it all

Holding on to what little he had, who knows how?

A false pride supporting him, he refused to bow

More out of rebellion than any solid ground

This was how his footing in life he'd always found

For when there is no love that is ever known

A void exists where nothing can be grown

To fill this space, the minds invention

He began to imagine a conspiracy, an intervention

No job, lost friend, no family to care

His only company was a mirror into which to stare

Day in, day out, a heavy sameness abounds

With lost dreams, all that remains are infertile grounds

We met by chance, I felt your pain

Though hidden behind a smile, it was there, an indelible stain

Why is Life so spare to some, their disappointments accumulate

He grew ever more committed to his unavoidable fate

But I'd seen his joy, when glimmers of hope shone through

When the prospects of a life no longer alone surfaced anew

Only to be dashed, more by his own dark hand

And find himself stranded in an all too familiar land

This hunger for love, to have in this world a place

And with it an identity, a home, an honest face

But when the hunger is too strong, and experience has taught

He never learned to trust, so alone everyday must be faught

There were times when I saw the seeds I'd planted begin to grow

When it seemed the chase would pause and some peace he
would know

But like some spectre surging up from deep inside

The beginnings of trust once again were thrust brutally aside

This most recent eruption cost him his last sanctuary

Back to the streets, the subway, though not yet the cemetary

So close to taking a fateful step towards a new start

It was hard to be helpless and watch him into the shadows dart

Into the night, like a thief alone

To sleep anywhere with sole companion a dead iPhone

No sun does he see, only cloudy skies

And people will always betray him with their lies

Trust is that hurdle he can't overcome

Whenever he gets too close to someone

He turns into a wild animal none can control

Once again two different people – not one whole

No one can survive torn thusly asunder

Neither side lasts – not the sun or the thunder

Flashes appear of good and bad

Moods swing from manic to sad

There are days when a hero from within him appears

To help the helpless, in these moments he knows no fears

It was the hero he'd wished for a thousand times

Who would save him from those dark mines

Better to save than to live abandoned to his fate

Saving others helped to fill his plate

He could be good, the world needed a hero

In those moments he could forget he lived as a zero

Arrested, hiding, ever on the run

It seems he feels safest as no one's son

I fear for his body, I fear for his mind

How long can he live in a world so unkind?

I told him to stay away, I'd done all I could

Demanding acknowledgement just how very good

I'd been to him, so he could no longer deny that trust can be

But there also a need for reciprocity

Not for me, I have no need of his gratitude

But if he is to continue, he must change his attitude

Others may want to help him on his way

And he must learn how "thank you" to say

Having turned the tables a bit to the right

He knows now the truth he'd kept out of sight

That running is now is a choice not his fate

And his life can begin again if he can lose his hate

I know Life has given him means denied to others

Who have not been cast aside by their fathers and mothers

There is indeed part of him I can never truly understand

One foot may be in my reality, but the other resides exclusively in his own land

So I hope these resources unknown to me

Can continue to provide him with the means of security

That his isolation won't dissolve that which holds him together

And allow him to survive the storm, and someday know a more clement weather

It saddens me so to see a life extinguish itself in a slow burn

Knowing how unlikely it may be that his world will ever turn

The seeds of his end were planted when he was so young

This lost boy unwanted, whose song went too long unsung

If there is a God who is loving and kind

Look down on this lonely heart, help him find

Some refuge where his flight can finally cease

And otherwise than in death, he can find some real peace.

EACH STEP

April 2010

Friday after tennis, shaken was your world

Into zones tempestuous you were hurled

Such harsh thoughts gathered, surrounding you

Chased the sun, leaving a troubled sky of murky blue

Such pain, such solitude, such doubt undeserved

Cure it my love could not, however unreserved

Difficult to watch you struggle as I know you did

The heart you showed me, it no longer hid

My pain for you, felt as I watch you hurt

With yourself the issues you do not skirt

Too harsh, too mean, too sharp, too raw

How to change this thing at your heart which does gnaw?

And yet, through your battles, I see progress you make

I feel your love, with each step that you take

Victory now - not yet the essential part

Feed your dreams, yourself, your love, your heart

The battle is now engaged, this I know

I've watched you these months, new seeds begin to grow

Progress never comes in a straight line

But strong and tall these seeds can grow over time

Prevail you will, even if now you doubt

When your heart aches and your head knows not what it's all about

One step at a time, though backwards you may think you go

Nothing can stop you, this I know

For you can love, I've tasted its glory

As you allow it - with great struggle - to rewrite your story

A tale long ago distorted, twisted into something wrong

Yet listen to the music you make today, it's your truer song

A cost I bear, a twofold bill

See you in pain then miss you still

Through our time together, I've learned to see beyond

The shallow waters of my subjective pond

You've given me a new reason to think beyond myself

To see something bigger than some self-absorbed elf

The one who in his self-pitying misfortune wallowed

There was more darkness than light, I risked being swallowed

Having you in my life, a warming focus I found

A glorious ship too long stuck in the ground

Take my love, my experience and whatever else of value that may be mine

I offer it willingly so make it thine

Your ship now risen from the mud – how fine

Watch the stars as they continue to align

And in so doing, if you will allow me so

I too learn, love, prosper and with you, grow

For the day will come when need you too I will

When in sorrow my own heart will need a refill

But together, as one, two stronger for sure

My ship, she of such beauteous allure

Will lift me up, when aground I may be

And carry me onwards to a calmer sea.

Return to your cave in these moments so dark

Live on stale water and cast off bark

If sustain you they have o'er these past many years

Then be grateful for their service, when they allayed your fears

But your life has changed, with new promise it's filled

The bear must seek refuge elsewhere, new fields call to be tilled

Not in the dark sad place from before

But in the sunlight, proud, happy, loved - that's what's in store.

These voices which turn good to bad

Which steal your smile and make you sad

Chase them away, see them for what they are

Cast them adrift, to float off to some foreign space far

Friends they are not, but demons they be

Distorting your thoughts and emotions, so as not to see

Words from the future tonight you may say

Not believing that yet has arrived that day

But the sun will come up, its light will fill your eyes

The only sound you'll hear, much relieved sighs

So do what you must now, do what you can

Know that you have no greater fan

Let me be your light, your knight, your hope

As through the darker moments you grope

I've no need to ask for promises unsound

For I know that which I have found

Find your way to a better space

And there, next to me will be waiting your place.

EACH AND EVERY DAY

July 14, 2012

What is love but that which draws us near?

That which defines who we hold dear

We learn these things as children from parents imperfect

And to protect ourselves, their love we often must deflect

A legacy from childhood to our adult years

They grow and own us, these ancient fears

A lifetime to cure these curses past

Only small steps can we manage, how they seem to last

Why is fear the stronger of the two?

Why these walls between me and you?

How am I different that to me they seem small?

And for you, they've grown so very tall?

Have I lived my life in such a different way?

That these fears hold on me such little sway

Was it the ocean I put between me and my past?

That they, not I, became the outcast

Or why have you, in spite of all you've done?

You believe you've lost far more than you have won

I think I will struggle with this in my search for love

When I seek a heart with whom to soar above

Each disappointment, each pair of empty eyes

Rekindles my lonely heart's forlorn sighs

Tormented no longer, moving again on my way

But I still think of you each and every day.

FANTASY

February 2016

This thing we call fantasy, so willingly embraced

Can its purpose, indeed its origins, be traced?

What starts as an image, charged with fascination

If indulged, can quickly become total domination

That which excites, calling to us from within

If followed blindly, contains the seeds of a serious sin

Not the literal kind, the harm others suffer at our hand

The one against ourselves, deforming our stand

Born of frustration, mixed with desire

The logs grow bigger, burning hotter always, the fire

No thirst is quenched when this hunger is sated

And the pleasure obtained, in truth, is grossly overrated

So what to make of this downward spiral?

Why has the internet made it go viral?

When all say they search but few seem to find

Emotion is lost as it all seems to unwind

The threads that bind, spun from caring and trust

All you hear talk of is some nut to bust

Unraveling the ball that connects us all

How can we avoid the inevitable fall?

The time when alone is all one can feel

No loving touch to warm, to heal

Will this age of emptiness come to an end?

Is that the message our troubled time does to send?

When the bubble bursts, imploding, devoid of air

When eyes finally open, from pain, made to once again care

But can one learn if never taught?

Can love be found if it has to be bought?

Something will happen, keep faith in some higher ideal

When the true meaning swings back from sensation to feel.

When hot and fun no longer rule

And to act like a tool makes one look like a fool

"Understanding does not cure evil, but it is a definite help, inasmuch as one can cope with a comprehensible darkness."

C.G. Jung

For those who believed that Jung was a spiritualist, an esoteric, lost in the collective unconscious, this simple statement shows just how pragmatic and grounded he was.

There is nothing magical or occult about human psychology. It is the story of how we got from there to here, and where we are going. Nothing is more comprehensible if one simply thinks about it.

FATHER'S DAY

June 2017

Today is Father's Day

What is it meant to say?

There is, of course, the social way

Indeed, What's that really meant to say?

To celebrate the one who sired us

To something typically masculine with little bother o fuss

A power tool, a handkerchief, a watch or a tie

All probably destined to end up in a closet or drawer – goodbye

For what can one offer to a father since most lived slightly effaced?

Mothers usually define them for children, since fathers too often live in haste

And so it goes on, a tradition sweet but lame

For there is little recognition of what lies behind a father's name

He went to work and paid the bills

Did he always take his pills?

Was he often sick or hurt?

Was he often angry and curt?

For his heart, his back, his neck, his knee

What is he? A man or a tree?

Coming back to the meaning of this day

Does it serve any purpose if we celebrate it this way?

Most father's have no clue how to express what to them it means

Perhaps because they've reflected too little, capturing only how it seems

From some sort of vague limbo, a cloud appears with no clear lines

More like a wild forest full of undergrowth and vines

Yet men are thought to see more clearly

Thinking in linear ways and neatly

But if they don't, if they only play their role

How significant is it to be one – and what's their goal

Ask the fathers you know, see what they say

They' probably speak of specific memories or a certain day

But their presence, was it felt during those precious childhood years?

When a father can do so much to allay a child's fears

So, incomplete, yet socially comparable

With little thinking, we act out some parable

And at the end of the day, we say goodbye

But was any real emotion shared – a smile or a good cry?

It makes sense if emotions float, like bubbles rising one at a time

That it's just another holiday with little meaning, and that's fine

But, if a Father saw his purpose in this role

If this was the path to being a man, and becoming whole

When Father's Day comes around

And it passes with hardly a sound

All those years when each facette was revealed

Bringing with it more depth, previously concealed

For we grow as circumstance commands

Embracing it or escaping to foreign lands

The former adds another answer to the question we all ask

Why am I here, and what is my task?

Does one need a day of recognition to make it real

Are medals to be handed out so proud one can feel?

I think not, for once pinned it's soon forgotten

Wrapped up carefully in some cotton

Put away in some night table drawer

Never to be thought of forever more

Unless on the day when he has come to pass

And everyone comes to honor his class

Realizing as they gather all to speak

They knew him but little, for he allowed but a peak

Was it humility or something less grand?

Did he think about things so he could take a stand?

Did he teach you anything lasting and deep?

Anything precious that you really want to keep?

HASTE

June 2017

Nowadays there's a nostalgia – declared – across much of the land

Lost, people feel, left behind with no solid ground on which to stand

Prophets, mostly false, claim they can turn back time

Back to the days when everything was fine

Even if that was never the case

There have always been issues of gender and race

Which excluded so many, forbidden the dream

Back then we could ignore them – until they started to scream

So a new imperative was thrust upon us

How to make room for everyone on the bus

Growth was declared the answer, just more of everything

And every man in his home, his castle could be once again king

And for awhile, growth we did know

More food, more things, more stuff, more money did flow

And with this prosperity, more people arrived by all sorts of means

Not all were capable of providing for themselves, budgets began busting at the seams

Then women finally were welcomed into the work force

Lucky them – along came child care costs, less time, failed marriages and divorce

And men hung on for awhile, fearing the worst

Too much supply in the labor force – soon to be cursed

Promotions dried up for all, litigation a threat

Political correctness dictated policy – a sure bet

And somewhere along the way, reality got lost

Worlds once stable got turned upside down and lives tossed

Whose fault was it? Has anyone even asked the question?

Like children, we look to parental figures, for reassuring explanation

Like parents not wanting to alarm their kids

The truth was avoided, and the pots kept their lids

In the simplest of terms where did we go wrong?

We preferred distraction and lies – a much catchier song

We forgot to ask the question – where did all of this growth come from?

Was there to be a cost down the road; what would be its sum?

Now it seems to me in a very simple expression

There are two forces at work here – let's make a minor digression

More people wanting more of everything

But could growth keep pace with those clamoring?

More prosperity, more cars, university degrees for the kids

It's simple, the numbers of people rose faster than growth – and so began the bids

Inflation came, prices had to rise

The economy grew, but fueled by inertia, not really by size

In relative terms, for the numbers told a different story

And as long as it looked good on paper, vive old glory

Until such time, as what had to happen occurred

And all of a sudden, confusion set in and our vision blurred

What really happened, and what's going on today?

Short and simple the answer – we've lost our way

We live in a finite world, with time measured as the universal constant

But our appetites must come from another dimension – distant

Where the laws of physics can be shaped to suit our taste

With no need to be concerned by devastation and waste

And thus began not the American Dream but the American Race

Instead of building slow and steady, we upped the pace

Sacrificing thoughtful measures in the name of haste

What we get wrong we could hide or fix, if not with concrete then cut and paste

And now what was due to happen has finally begun to arrive

Most everyone is running, trying to survive

It's an old story for its happened before

Though then it ended in war, blood and gore

Our means to resolve conflicts so far have held

Though ignoring them as we've done, roads and bridge have been felled

Our structures of government now tested though stressed

What should we do – cling to the old notion that we are by definition still "the best?"

Does that solve any problem, fix any road?

Argue with one another, each other in conflict we goad

Resentment, that child of ignorance with its fantasies that try to explain

Why things are different now from before and why we're "suddenly" in such pain

How did this happen? It can't be my fault

Let's find an easy target – whatever it is we must halt

Will that work – many believe that it will

Once bought the snake oil lasts only until

The whole things falls down, there are no more lies

No more fantasies or apple pies in the skies

We're a strong people – or at least we were

We'll just have to stop with the self satisfied purr

Who calls for us to take a giant step back?

To ponder our errors, and fill in the crack

To start fresh, if that's what's required

To get us out of this swamp in which we're now mired

To learn to live in this world with which we are blessed

With measured thought and humility – and stop thumping our chest

To nurture what we could so easily lose

Is there still enough wisdom in this world to choose?

A path of reason, of thought and learning

Instead of more cars or designer shoes – for which we've been yearning

Slow down the pace of life, "busyness" carries the seeds of destruction

Our minds, our children, our culture is on the path of deconstruction

To disassemble in a few decades what's taken millennia to build

Sure we've paid a high cost on the way, so much suffering, so many killed

Is that the endpoint of all the greatness that came before?

To land here in a time when intelligence is considered a bore

To step into mindlessness and close behind us oblivion's door

And start each day what we've learned from the past to ignore

Reinventing what we knew, claiming it as ours

Reinventing history not in terms of years but hours

Deprived of what came at such a high cost

I shudder at the new ignorance, so much is lost

If we cling to the notion, as the best, we'll always end up on top

Stop for a moment to consider what the world could look like if it all went "**POP!**"

If you think you're in bad shape now, having lost so much

Set aside this false sense of security – you are out of touch

This land of the hero, the individual alone as master of his fate

Who through his own efforts piled high with riches his plate?

Ignores something essential in this arrogant act

This nation provides the foundation – and that's a fact

You want to defend something of value, leaving more than you found

Pause for long enough to see our current direction – look around.

We've had a nice run with some bad and much good

It doesn't have to be over if we've finally understood

The world has changed in ways we don't comprehend

But if we chose the past, tooth and nail to defend

The outcome is certain, unwittingly we'd have chosen not to win

Would that not be the greatest sin?

So pardon my lengthy digression, always so much to say

Take it for what it's worth, let my thoughts nourish your day'

Reflect on the fruit of what I've tried to assemble

With a slightly new perspective – if so honored – look to a wiser future then with no need then to tremble.

IT It COULD HAPPEN HERE

February 2017

We live in times strange and unexpected

Though our nations, democratic, officials we elected

Yet shifts of potentially tectonic force

Have riven once unified polities, we now face divorce

What were these forces, subterranean yet strong

That made us forget how we managed to get here, and why we belong

Not to one another, but to something greater

Some sense of us, apparently disguised the crater

The one that was forming beneath our feet

The one we need to take seriously, or face defeat

For what has emerged, without no one anticipating its timing or force

Harkens to a darker time, if one only looks, unafraid, of course

For to see a danger coming requires courage and more

The more terrifying the danger, and what might lie in store

Frightens us so we prefer not to see

That if we don't stop it, what will come to be

These moments of opportunity, let's call them so

Arrive not by chance, the stars align slowly into what we will come to know

It might be some shift, subtle but sure

Not seen as a challenge, at first, to what we believe will always endure

Then another crack appears in the foundations of our state

Seeds of doubt take root, even if the danger seems to abate

See, we reassure ourselves, it was nothing at all

How could such a small thing threaten a fall?

For we built this nation, one we believe to be great

To last 1000 years – sound familiar? – this remarkable state

For it is the reflection of who we think we are

And in truth, looking back, we have indeed come far

So easy to take credit for things we weren't around to make

When we replace truths with myths, flatteringly fake

Ask anyone what was the secret blend

What allowed us to survive our wounds, heal and mend

To grow strong, the strongest, when all others did to fail

Alone we rose up, the Eagles head, but not his tail

We have forgotten the element, the glue, that held it together

That allowed us to endure the vagaries of wars and weather

There was, indeed, a sense of individualism; self reliance made us strong
Frontiersmen, adventurers, farmers all part of one nation to which

they did belong

But can a single person, only by himself, a nation build?

And welcome others to this land, contributing to its coffers filled?

Can each individual do this on his own?

Or have we forgotten? Let the truth be known

What was created by one man, lord of all he might see

Is the work or hubris and lack or humility

Myths are created, a culture's story to tell

Some survive the centuries, even if empires fell

We marveled at their achievements, as if we understood

Why some we remember, others we forget – be they evil or good

A whitewash occurs, an embellished version is sold

Dissent is discouraged, lead is turned to gold

Life laughs at such things, as we strive for what should not be ours

We build monuments to ourselves, with steeples and tall towers

We reach for the sky, as the myth makes its rounds

Numbed by the senseless chatter and other distracting sounds

Cities flourish, along with towns

Often drunk in their glory which abounds

Until that twist of fate settles on their grounds

That's when men's mettle is tested, when reality sounds

Doubt seeps in. How did this all come to pass?

Is this the endpoint, or only a passing morass?

The future is ours to dream. Then we must make it so

Nations reflect their people's worth – no preordination can they
Know

To make us great again – when were we ever really that?

It's not enough to repeat it constantly to turn it into fact

And looking for some tautology which cannot be understood

Tell me, why would that bring anything of good?

Anchoring reality in some ancient book

Written by who knows who, tall tales from the past they took

Or even a legal document, brilliant for sure

Requires often a periodic second look if it is to endure

Nothing written long gone can resist the change of time

Some values may be immutable, but none are forever divine.

Question we must always, as the world continues to evolve

Copernicus was right – around the earth the Sun does not revolve

If an anchor you require, one that cannot shift

Resist change and you will surely be cast off and set adrit

Though we are fallible, we've proven it time and time again

That's why we write history with paper, ink and pen

Spoken words and stories telling of time past

Can only suffer changes, unchanged they never last

The only things that can keep us safe – from ourselves and the Unknown

Are the fruit of our own efforts and the seeds we will have sown

If we act as honest brokers and never trade in truths that are for real

Share we must some portion of reality to preserve the commonweal

Our tools, imperfect, can temper when our minds are deceived

There's perhaps another truth, one which must be believed

Remembering this world belongs to no one and why we are here

Our time here is short , our mission great, bring courage and not fear

Our purpose: to watch over all creation, all things great and small

For if we fail in this, how mighty will be our fall.

LEADERSHIP

May 2017

Much discussion of leadership of late

When the people must chose a nations fate

How do they approach the moment of decision?

On what will they base their choice, reason or derision?

What do they know of how the government works?

Are they responsible citizens or just self absorbed jerks?

Have they followed the things that have transpired?

Or were they just too lazy to be inspired?

And what have they heard from all the words that were spoken?

Did they ponder the full question or just bitch how the system was broken?

For much is wrong the way things have evolved

Yet how many were truly involved?

How big is their world, what counts the most?

Is it really all about me, and all I want is to coast

Through life, happy with money to spend?

Is there anything but my comfort that I am prepared to defend?

And what of the others, who share this land?

For whom will I raise my voice and take a stand?

The poor? What do I really think?

Is there a bigger picture or should I just let them sink?

Is it their fault, all they have to do is try?

This land of exception and opportunity, is that the answer I buy?

And the sick who drive my premiums higher?

Do I want to understand why or am I denier?

Do I listen with but one ear, with a filter on top?

All these meaningless buzz words, I just want it to stop

A leader, someone who can fix it for me

Someone who I recognize, with whom eye to eye we see

But what did he say, I don't really recall?

Just that he would make it better, I think that's all

But isn't that all I care to know, learning is so hard?

This coming weekend we'll have a big barbecue in the yard

Maybe we'll argue about baseball and such

There aren't many things, after all, that interest me that much

He seems to be angry that life is passing me by

We all say we work hard, (really?) life is good, why should I have to try?

From my cozy place in this world, even if things change, why should I have to cry?

Let someone else worry, why the hell should I

Take it from someone else, the lazy bunch

I'm hungry. What's on? Let's order in for dinner and lunch

When did we grow so disconnected?
Are we really all that disaffected?
That nothing really matters except me
Or has it already happened and I choose not to see?

Life is hard, unpredictable with surprises around the bend
No one can tell you with any certainty how it might end
There is more than just tomorrow or one week from now
Who will provide for my future, with what and how?

We've filled our heads with lies, rendered deaf, dumb and blind
And worst of all, I've conceded the very use of my mind
Dedicated to futile pursuits
Fun with the boys. Laughs. Hoots

Has it gone this far, ignorance my new creed
As long as I can indulge my appetites, what else do I need
But my mind is the only tool I truly possess
It's time to grow up and seriously confess

We've delegated what's really sacred, our role in this world

As long as we sing the anthem at football games with the flag unfurled

Have we fulfilled our citizens'' mission?

Now pass me the remote, what's on the television?

If Trump was elected – though explanations abound

The one overriding answer that none can confound

The one that no one has spoken of to date

It's so much easier to vote with one's gut and a heart full of hate

To point the finger elsewhere, we always need another to blame

We've grown fearful of getting too close to the truth's flame

The answer is clear, look yourself in the face

And ask yourself simply, standing quietly in place

No distractions, no cell phone, no meetings, no noise

Have we collectively not acted like one of those good old boys?

We believe without knowing, taking the easy way

I just want to have fun and get on with my day

Why worry, I live in a disposable time?

Leaders who disappoint me, they won't get any vote of mine

Is that all there is, that's how much I have come to care?

Seen this way, as a nation, how can well can we fare?

The problem isn't leadership in this nation of sheep

The problem is us, we've all fallen asleep

It's happened to others – Italy 's a good case

We are surely not immune, it's just a matter of pace

They say in democracy, one gets the leaders one deserves

And the future that emerges, no surprises, it reserves

So predictable, if only we care to look

There no magic, it's as clear as if written in a book

Sure, events can erupt, having a mind of their own

But the plants that grow come from the seeds that are sown

In this land drunk on its' exceptionalism

That feeds on few facts, but more on derision

If the picture I've drawn feels too close to what's real

If it's all about me, and for others I don't really feel

If I believe my success come from me alone

If I should get the whole roast, including the bone

Caring nothing for all that keeps me afloat

What can happen to this big old boat?

The one that we're on, raping it with no thought

At some time we'll run out; and have to face the future we bought?

So here's the question, from the wealth we were given

Maybe we made the most of it, with ambition we've striven

Forgetting only, we sink or we swim, all as one

It's not about money, power or even fun

It's as old fashioned as putting differences aside

Seeing the truths by which others abide

Not as wrong, but motivated by values and choice

But have we all thought it through, or just repeated another's voice

That sounded good in the moment, easy to buy it whole

With no evidence that it will work, and what might be the toll

Leaders emerge reflecting their time

Jumping on board in the moment they may seem fine

But if that's what you've done with no sense of the why and the how

Aren't they then just another idol to which we bow?

I thought, in your system, that this was wrong

Are you a simple chorus repeating lines in some song?

Who are you, do you think, have you truly understood?

Or, in fact, you don't really care?   Now how is that good?

MEN

May 2017

Some months ago, or was it years

I noted a change in men and their fears

There were, of course, the obvious ones

Confused on how to be husbands, fathers and sons

Battered by shifts in their gender roles

No mythical challenges to face – no mountains, only knolls

Or so it seemed; no inspiration stirred their souls

No means to grow into stallions from foals

For each in his way, to feel oneself a man

A quest is required, his soul's fires to fan

To feel the difference that defines

And tap into that source that HE can mine

The vein runs deep, filled with wealth

Exploited in the open or with stealth

To stand for something he knows is right

Something able to withstand the scrutiny of the brightest light

To do his part, whatever that may be

It's the only path to set him free

From the past when he was but a child

Or even an adolescent, incomplete and wild

To take the step into this role

To discover that which will make him whole

Responsibilities embraced are first required

To step out of the playroom, ambitions fired

To strive for more than just fun and games

To have something more to say than calling others names

To see a purpose, a direction that makes sense

One that can survive the present tense

Why give up one's freedom to provide and protect?

When the panoply of distractions awaits, one need only sele

tThat is the key, no other is real

It's a purpose, a role greater than oneself one must feel

Giving up something trivial for something that will last

Steady and sure, purposeful, considered, not fast.

Only then does a boy become a man

He can stand alone, not be just a fan

On this ground, solid and true

The page is turned to reveal a life that is new

Where what biology has decided, the place it did start

Ensures nothing of his future part

Multiple auditions in those early years

Reveal much of those trials and the many fears

For a boy is a man who has yet to discover

His strength, his courage and his ability to recover

From the blows Life delivers, at the time making no sense

Yet when taken together many years hence

Relate the story of how he came to be

Did he face his demons or join the enemy?

For the true undoing of most every man alive

Is how he abandoned himself, forgetting to strive

To become what good fortune offered, to become something more

In looking ahead to see but a door

Will his first thought be to wonder what lay behind?

Will there be some treasure waiting there for him to find?

This is a version, in the classic sense

Has it changed so much in this present tense?

And what of the future, where will it lead?

Will there be men or boys, complete or in need?

The journey demands a depth, a reason

For a lifetime and not just a season

And to guide the way, is that not why Father' exist?

To provide a pathway and the strength to resist

The trials that await all boys

To develops their tools and abandon their toys

To build whatever they need to feel validated

And not get lost in the confusion that has so many negated

No diatribe for or against any choice

If life is to be a celebration where all can rejoice

ust beware getting caught up in a wave

For the sea is a dangerous place, from where it's hard to save

This is no simple matter done once and for all

To be a boy is to admire a man, one who stands tall

So easy to get lost along the way

The choice is each one's, political correctness must not hold sway

For some this may be little more than sedition

It's all genetic, now our national tradition

Ask yourself this if you are of such a mind

Would you rather play no role in choosing your kind?

There too, which way would a boy choose to go?

Too young and inexperienced, and if unguided, unable to know

The collective "we" now wants to speak with one voice

So sign up, get in line, what's this about individual choice?

And a man, how would he this situation face

With experience of himself, his family, and his race

For a man makes his choices alone, knowing why

He samples life first, giving all things a try

And then once informed, a thoughtful time

To decide which road he will embrace as mine

Not just to belong to the "other" club, different from the one rejecting

How does that solve anything, if but a surrogate reflecting

Exaggerations of attributes misunderstood

Bigger and better – however thoughtless – must be good

This band aid can serve as but a palliative

Is that really how anyone wants to live?

But now our modernity inclusive of all

Men seem not to know who they are and what's the cal

l

To be strong and assertive, powerful in all things

But also sensitive, vulnerable, emotionally open – kings?

What a choice, what's the new ideal?

Pulled in opposite directions, can he keep an even kee

l

Role models may change, somewhat in tune with now?

But if the essential is lost, the question remains – how?

Why some might ask, do we need a male when genders blend

Are we ready Nature's constitution to amend?

What messages do Fathers send?

Preferences may change, but can gender really bend?

In the past it was a search which was an essential part

What one discovered along the way revealed what was missing at
the start

The pieces merged together forming a whole

Never perfect is Life, but there was a way forward and a role

But today, will there be no answer but only doubt?

No thought of what might be learned and what it is all about

Caring more for the tethers that bound but also kept him safe

When he was a child and the tethers did not yet chafe

We speak not of ambition, blind and greedy

Fed by anger and crushed dreams of the damaged or emotionally
needy

Though these days we know more of this kind

And what of the others of a different mind?

We used to nourish a vision of men

Defined as heroes – stronger than any ten

Was it innocent, naïve, maybe we needed to believe

Some sense of the inferior it was meant to relieve

Then came a time when the image was turned inside out

We saw their underside: bumbling, inept, filled with doubt

More human they were called, this side we did need to see

Those heroes from before were not real, mostly fantasy

But has their time gone on too long?

Loners, tormented, damaged, they don't belong

Now we've actually got one in charge

Like a bull in a china shop, in he does barge

Showing all the things men are not meant to be

Thinking his purpose is to unleash disruption indiscriminately

Inflicting his pain, hidden unsuccessfully

On those around him – he is nobody

It's time to reconsider, to bring them both home

Neither is useful when existing alone

To forge the two back into one

When balance will return to the Sun.

Aggression. Violence. Insensitivty – so cruel

Who would choose such an option? Only a fool?

There is no denying the harm that's been done

Is this where it ends or has it only begun?

All things grow, evolve, building on the past

Recalling the harm ensures the memory will last

All things must have a foundation

Chaos precedes all meaningful creation.

Now not every man is destined a hero to be

Those bigger than life, there for all to see

But there is something essential that all men should share

The strength that comes when is felt the need to care

Is this the new man, caring for what's bigger than he?

When he can choose by himself and thusly feel truly free

When the horizon is seen high in the sky

And he can dream again bigger, but most of all try.

If not then backwards we go

Literally every man for himself, imagine the show

Not forward into some future equal and bright

But lost, frightened and confused, back into the night.

NARCISSUS REDUX

August 2015

Remember him?

He who's principal sin

Or so we understood

Cared only for himself, ignoring the good

The story went that a glance at his reflection was enough

To dismiss all the rest, concerned with only self-centered fluff

But was so taken by his own visage

Was that the real explanation for falling in love with a mirage?

As we so often do here, in this land of simplicity

We look no further, satisfied with superficiality

For there are always reasons for the things that we do

We'd just rather not bother, and so what if we knew

Now there's another question, more specific this time

Is there any sense to knowing ourselves when I've decided I'm fine

When all I do is right, I can bear no blame

So why ask when the answer will always be the same?

A strange starting point for a nation on psychiatric drugs

But maybe that's the point, a constant numbness can block out the bugs

It was said long ago only an examined life is worth living

But with all our toys and taste for distraction, why bother with misgivings?

It is what it is – I don't really care

Since there's nothing I can do, just to myself I'll be fair

Why bother with others – there's only time for me

To the point that they cease to figure in my equation, now that sets me free

So in the face of resignation and randomness, the new God of causation

Let's just have fun – and of course work – what a happy nation

I have my toys, my distractions, my markers for success

So everyone else can see just how much I've been blessed

By the Great God Jobs, the Lord of distraction

Enabling more fun – no longer just a fraction

Of the time I might have spent listening to the voices from inside

Instead of heeding their warnings, I can now block them and
effectively hide

But who am I hiding from, and why is that so

Since everything is wonderful here stateside, this we all by definition
we know

Who needs to see things others have done

How could they possibly be better off and having more fun?

I've got the latest iPhone, Instagram, Snapchat and apps galore

What could I be missing – but somehow life has become a bore

So I've turned to sex – perhaps the last recreational resort

Every teenage boys fantasy – several times a day to cavort

I'm hot. She's hot – could it be any better?

Maybe I'll go shopping – I could use a new sweater.

But what was her name again, and I've just shown her the door

Was fun doing it for the first time on the floor

Back online, not really sated, though orgasmically so

But why then is it like a bowel movement, I can use any toilet – even
the one's I don't know

Have you ever made love? Don't look at me that way?

Fucking isn't sex – just kindergarten free play

For it's a verb describing what one does to another

But where is the sharing, the connection – better chase those
questions and find some other

Has it started to sink in, where this can only end

Another pesky question, who cares what I might intend

Don't really have the answer myself to that one

So back to Tindr to find some more fun

If corporations are people – as Romney has said

Then people are but second class citizens, and might as well be
dead

Thank God we're allowed these distractions aplenty

For with eyes wide open heaven knows what we'd see

A world emptied of substance, filled rather with things

Where words like growth, investment, capital, inflation – these are
the new Kings

Yet if that is the case, why am I here?

What purpose can I serve, and who are these strangers I have sex with but fear

I've never taken the time, too busy with my things

Someone else can answer the doorbell when – and if – it ever rings

So who is Narcissus, not a person but a mask

That's the last question he'd ever want me to ask

Where is he in his development, from child to boy to man?

Is he capable of anything of consequence, can he take a stand?

If all that ever counted was his glorious self

Why is no one beating down his door leaving him on some paltry shelf

Perhaps – just perhaps – he's not such a wonder

And those trophies he's got are in fact a terrible blunder

All those empty words of praise from parents too busy and absorbed to cast a gaze

Lost their son is, as if in a maze

This child, needs to build a view

To understand what's important, what's old, and what's new

For now, all he knows is Job's latest iphone

For others to see and to know he's someone, not just another gnome

Why do men grow from little boys to so much more?

How do they view the futures' challenges and know what's in store

And do they believe their fate they can mold

And what does that word mean – in little use nowadays – bold

We are born to be tested, to question and learn

To win and fail, to soar and crash and burn

How else to truly know what I am worth

If Mommy and Daddy fix all my problems, it's all a fantasy, fun and mirth

Or is it really, for when – God forbid – I am alone

No iPod, no iMac, no iWatch, no iPhone

There are voices whispering words of fear and doubt

Against which I have nothing to counter that has any clout

So cling to my image, the reflection by my parents given to me

I can do no wrong, and it's enough just to be

But be what? Be who? Towards what end? And how to proceed?

If I'm empty I must take from others, voila – the birth of greed

It's only those with something of substance inside

From those voices they've got answers, they've no need to hide

And how is the visible, how can we know

With each responsibility, our roots reach deeper, and thus we grow

A boy thinks only to play. A teenager thinks only his thoughts –
others have nothing to say

And the young man, who should be ready to set out to seek his fate

He lives at home, Mom does his wash, and when after eating, no
thought to wash his plate

It's she who in the morning must ensure he is not late

Sad are these young people robbed of confidence and a life

Their focus is career, money, more things, sex – but no wife

For a wife implies caring for someone new

Is it possible they might be just as important as you?

And then there's the children – OMG – there's already no time for
me

I'll pay someone else to raise them, there, that's fine, we'll all be
happy

GROWTH, GOD AND WAR

June 2017

This is a story as old as the world

It's evolved as human time has unfurled

Though the lives we now live resemble naught

So many bloody battles it seems we've faught

What have we learned that its now replaced?

That single-minded striving to win with its bitter after taste

Men being of the bigger stronger kind

Though size it seems, has had little effect on our mind

Hide it, dress it up, clothe it however you like

Cruel and uncaring we came into this world, ready to strike

No matter how small or great the group which was ours

Whether we lived in huts or high towers

Be it for women, goats, water or gold

It's always been the same story that's been told

First comes competition for resources rare

After we've raped the land until it's bare

Followed by conflict, it's natural mate

Along with its motor – anger and hate

Wrongs committed, whether true or false

It's always the vilification of the other, the same dance, the same waltz

If we look at ourselves, we are all the same

We even go by this collective name

Now associate it with some higher power

And look upon the "others" as we prepare for the holy hour

When the wrong shall be righted, what was taken, returned

And in the process, who really cares what to the ground has been burned?

To the victor the spoils, it's the rule of war

The defeated count but for little, they deserve what's in store

The weapons have improved, they kill with precision and ease

MAD is the only failsafe we now have, and it's quite the tease

Now stop for a moment, this to consider

What's the raw material, the fodder that goes to the highest bidder?

If war requires men in ever increasing numbers

We need soldiers, carpenters, chemists and plumbers

But if men become soldiers, whose to replace?

Once war begins, it can start to look a lot like a race

The raw material of war is the sons fathers made

Preferred by the military to girls, they're stronger and thought to be more staid

When facing conflict, they've been raised to believe

Their numbers must be sufficient the casualties to relieve

Is this the true value we still implicitly place on men in our time?

Is this the best we can hope for? Keep them coming in line?

What of reason? Is competition the only choice?

I think part of the equation is missing – where is its voice?

We live in a world that is finite and real

As our numbers increase is there no choice but to steal?

Whatever the system, whatever it pretends

Competition's child - conflict and tears. It doesn't mend

So we've come up with the concept long ago

It's a canny expression, fooling even those who claim to know

Growth is the answer, that's all we need do

If a rising tide lifts all boats, why are the rich so few?

If our numbers grow faster than growth itself

And we're more numerous to share in this finite wealth

The answer seems clear, so simple to me

The only thing destined to grow is poverty

Growth lives in this world of limits and borders

Sooner or later we'll push against all peaceful world orders

And once that happens, forces beyond our control

Light a fuse that will take a terrible toll

I don't think I'm naïve or a fool of some sort

I play tennis so I understand the limits of a court

Within the lines, there are rules, I can do all I am capable of

The competition is inherent, but funny they included the term "love"

It means zero – what a lovely idea

It softens the blow and with it the fear

To be serious again, we need to understand

Perhaps possession has gained the upper hand

We are here but for so short a time

Yet we spend our lives accumulating things, so we can call them mine

And when I'm gone, what's passed along?

More things to own, to protect, to fight over – to our children's they now belong

An inheritance, that's great, wealth I didn't earn

Now I can spend what I want, cash to burn

To buy more things, to forget what counts

That's a terrible legacy if it's to that it amounts

This is how all conflicts begin and endure

Passed from one generation to the next – that's for sure

It's certain there is a right and a wrong – justice exists somewhere

In a place that's abstract with a tenuous link to what's fair

And there are times when arms must be taken up to defend the weak

To abandon them to fate comes with a cost, they must also speak

And we must listen, and think long and hard

Must there really be a fence in every yard?

Is competition at the root of it all

Why must we teach our sons to heed its call?

Objections aside, there is an "us" to defend

But before we unleash the forces, and bombs to send

Pause for just long enough to see the big picture

And forget about God and his holy scripture

Do we need to be sanctioned by some sacred power

Who will ensure our victory, from on high he will glower

And make our foe fall to our force

Really? This sounds more like the ass end of a horse

Even set aside for a moment, the chores waiting in the yard

To forget just how important this is shouldn't be so hard

To drown out the truth in some cold beer's carbonated fizz

Would to do so mean the end of us, no matter what is?

We'd have ended up where we began, in that same old muddy ditch.

Damn, life sure can be a bitch......

WE WASTE SO MUCH

July 15, 2012

As time passes and the days go by

The road shortens as the end draws more nigh

Though still a distant vision, a ghost

What remains ever present is what I miss the most

Oft I've said it to little effect

The portent is too heavy, carefully held in check

All that we have is the time we are given

And waste so much of it, by pointless ends and illusions are we driven

Distraction rules our daily world thus filled

The minutes, the hours fly by as life is slowly killed

Rather than cherish this precious thing

Rather than see the truth, hear its ring

Futile endeavors, the essential is lost

So much joy drains from our lives; a terrible cost

I cannot charge others; my discovery came in life late

My earlier years were more blind, emptier my true plate

But now that vision has returned to my eyes

Now my heart has learned to see through the lies

And though much was done in the times gone by

An emptiness has surfaced, driving me to try

For once to know the flavors of joys shared

All else pales when to it is compared

So in spite of it all, that which I've tried

Even if love to me has often lied

I heard its' words, the magic it brought

Like some bird in a net, I've found myself caught

But the capture was sweet and I took a step

Though never in your arms have I slept

Lies were told, that was clear

But always, I can still feel you near

The net has fallen away and I am once again free

To roam this world in search of another thee

With eyes open now, able more clearly to see

I go from flower to flower like some hungry bee

If it were given to me to define

How would I want to live my remaining time

With whom would I share all I really have that is mine

Would I once again sign on the dotted line?

No document this time, no legal pact

Together is enough, two hearts, a fact.

 Free from convention, I am my own man

To search, to try, passions flames to fan

Yet each equation, complex and rich

Requires two hearts, therein lies the hitch

For love is early ruled by winds wild and unknown

We may have lived, but how much have we grown?

At times, it seems, vision comes too late

When one has eaten many meals from a unclean plate

But if one has lived, sincere, as the search has progressed

Even the missteps, at the end, provide clarity, thusly blessed

Soiled souls, tired, disillusioned, battered and lost

Reborn from their innocence, another chance, wisdom acquired at great cost

Should the essence dissolve into the ether, recognizable no more?

Then little hope remains for what is in store.

So mind your heart as you stumble through life

As you struggle to choose wisely and deal with the strife

For blind we are born, and for too long blind we live

Forgetting which is more important, to take or to give

The first lives closeby, insecurity its voice

The hollow feeling that results, drives every future choice

But to give, what to make of that?

More often it reminds me of passing the hat.

Of giving to the poor, those without

Why should I care? What's that about?

Giving has roots lying far deeper inside

Our better angels from whom we too often seek to hide

What's in it for me, the new aside

The one we hear whispered in a tone most snide

Greed, avidity, envy, mistrust

Las Vegas – heaven? Win the big prize or bust?

No building, no small steps, no reflection for me

On top of the world – or nothing – that's what I see

How often does that happen, and even if it may

The benefits slip through greedy fingers, not long does it stay.

But the giving, that which comes from the essence of who we could be

To be in touch with the inner wealth we don't often see

No one taught me how else to be

Why are so few thus learned and free?

Success is defined by others unnamed

How is it our nature they have so easily tamed?

Did we abandon our souls on hearing the call?

Or born empty, anyway headed to the fall?

The mountain we climb to its very peak

Not realizing until then it's too late to speak

Those words of caring, making me see

There is a me only if a you there be

Alone the silence, the darkness of some roiling sea

If you'd but realized I have more only if more I can give to thee.

Could the blinders have been lifted, allowing you to see

Not just all I had to give, but all that you could be.

SERIOUSLY?

June 2017

Seriously. An expression commonly used

It implies that some convention has been abused

And with irony, the perpetrator is served a dose of disdain

Though unlikely some reflection to provoke, it can cause at least
some pain

Our discourse has evolved, implying no direction

Personally, my sense is it's more of a regression

Social interaction, a technical name

For the obvious exchanges which define the human game

How have things devolved so? Some examples might serve

Have you noticed that honesty no longer receives the respect it
deserves?

Exaggeration, obfuscation, flat out lies

All have grown more permissible affecting little our ties

To others, who used to compose our universe large and small

When we are all more or less the same, few conflicts did befall

Thanks to this convention, the world assumed some order

Rules were established, shared across every border

Of late has come other words that flow from with such ease

Innovation, change, progress – could they hide some disease?

Not in and of themselves, a singular thought

The problem is that no one cares much when wholesale they are
bought

Innovation implies the end of that which came before

Rendering outmoded products still on shelves in the store

We can sell them at a loss or just give them away

What happens to those affected? Have they had their day?

Retrain, reallocate, reeducate, reassign or just retire?

Those touched can't just be thrown in the fire

Too old, lacking the foundation. Who will pay?

No one in authority has the solution, but this they cannot say.

Next up is change, the master of our fate

Better to embrace it full heartedly or ignore your expiration date

But what is change? What does it look like?

Someone please explain to me. Please pick up the mike

Corporate buzz words abound- technical terms designed to confuse

Buying time to pull the rug out and keep the truth out of the news

It's clear, however, that change must come

Can it be planned to protect those affected before it's begun?

Or rather let's announce it with a clarion call

Harken back to the need to innovate or we will fall

Frighten the population into some form of submission

And turn those who protest its speed with high minded derision

For in the name of progress, anything can be sold

The future belongs not to the meek but the bold

And Capitalism with is all knowing free markets and stock exchange

Will solve all our problems – a tautology that should derange?

Markets may rule when there is no limit to time

We can pick our frame of reference and chart some line

To suit our numbers so they look just fine

And the argument is proven through some quantitative design

So imbued with the sheer size of the numbers we face

Who can keep up? When did thinking become a race?

Forge ahead, we can fix it later

Beware those who want to slow down – the progress hater

Who longs for a justice that implies taking from me

And give to others, how's that fair? I don't see.

The needy, the sick, the foreigners too numerous

When did they get here? I don't find this humorous

For this is a white Christian nation

With our self-proclaimed work ethic (now please the ovation)

We may work more hours, but not by choice

With the demise of the unions, we've lost a necessary voice

My success, my wealth – all the fruit of my labor

No one helped me, I had no helper, no savior

In this land which honors those who deserve

All that's mine I want to keep for myself in my personal reserve

These others, like parasites, who don't want to work

Freeloaders, thieves, rapists, jer

The send us their sick and we pay for their care

Raising our own costs, how do they dare?

A wall might help to keep them out

The Chinese have a big one. Did it work? This I doubt

Anger our friends, confuse them all

They owe us so much money, why must we alone carry the ball?

The result? A world in disarray

Who's in charge? What to think? What to say?

I'll listen to the media, they speak as if they know

Seriously? Will they inform me so my mind can grow?

There it is. The word that started this rhyme

It's gone better than I thought and took less time

Current events have seized me, I am no longer free

But there are days when I'd rather close my eyes than see.

For the problem is not the goon in the house so white

Who is deluded in all things, for he must be right

It's those who suspended their intelligence, chose ignorance in its place

And when his image appears, they should really see their own face

A symptom of some malaise which has infected our nation

The direction we've chose will lead to no salvation

All we can hope for is the absence of any major disaster

And if you know how to speed up the clock, *please, make it go faster.*

BOYS TO MEN

July 2017

Since human time began

And after woman men ran

Certain things have set them apart

Though violent at times, each knew their part

Men were to display certain traits

Designed to open the gates

To hunt, to fight, to protect and provide

And often to hit and run away to hide

Strength was required along with skill

Even after the advent of farming, they would kill

Defend what was theirs as best they could

And build homes and heat fires made of wood

Aggression, competition, at times selfish and cruel

Ambitious at times, always more to rule

More women, more land, more beasts of the field

Always wanting more, all things must increase their yield

Much has changed since these earliest of days

And men have adopted far more civilized ways

But the core of what it is to be a man

Is basically to do all that you can

An imperative rooted somewhere deep in their soul

Though not automatic, there is a road to becoming whole

A boy is born and is told what he is to become

Regardless of his nature, he must be his father's son

What that means is rarely clear

And often engenders in the son no small amount of fear

Some fathers are worth, others are not

They offer no path to follow, are a blot

A space that requires something within

It can be so filled by virtue or sin

For what is it that makes a man different from others of his kind

Is it only his size, his strength, or is it something else – perhaps his mind

For a man is that he does, not the words he speaks

These values that guide him always, not just weeks

They derive themselves from certain traits

That must be discovered and nurtured over time as he waits

For the moment when curiosity arrives

And starts to define the things for which he strives

To leave his home, his family and all they provide

To venture out into the wide world, not hide

To discover his courage when danger is faced

To know fear and to face it, his demons embraced

This all comes together, his passage to his manhood

To know the difference, and abandon the bad for the good

These journeys are part of the human story

Often filled with scenes scarey and gory

But this is the only way to know

How to be a man, and make it so

Some are lucky, providence watches over and can endow

Boys who have real fathers guide them and thusly allow

An easier time, making a place for them in the world of men

Easing the passage as the time arrives when

An inner strength is found, they can stand on their own

Owning their virtues, and for their sins, atone

Others, less fortunate, have a harder way

No one to guide them and for this there is a price to pay

Some fall victims to evil elders perverse

Who alter their course not for the better but for the worse

Harder to find the guide when none volunteers

Harder to find one's courage and to confront one's fears

Some succeed, some do fail

Some sing songs, others in silence wail

So it has been for a long long time

But in the end, there was always a straight line

Yet of late a change has occurred which challenges this way

Women have discovered they can and do deserve their say

But if that which separates the genders too

How does a boy know what to do

No longer in need of protection from man or beasts

No longer in need of wealth, she can pay for her own feasts

No longer someone to be responsible for her fate

She can take him or leave him and simply just wait

If these were the arms by which boys became men

The signs on the road have fallen down, though we don't know when

But what we can know, what we can see

That boys have a harder time men to be

Has the train gone off the tracks or simply taken a new route

Whatever the answer, I see to many who pout

No longer seeing the need to proceed

Courage has slowly been replaced by greet

For without these things which make men real

Regardless of their size, their strength, their feel

It's only when aligned with something bigger than themselves

They will always stay little boys, mischievous elves.

What remedy exists that can right the ship?

One can't go back in time, an impossible trip

To look forward means to look into the unknown

To do that courage – and a real pair must be grown

Of course, I speak in the metaphorical sense

But if one were to judge by just how tense

And uncertain, for reasons of context, not just gender

To be truly brave one must know how to care and be tender

Violence and brutality, often thought masculine traits to be

Requiring the confines of civilization to tame them – a fantasy

More a matter driven by fear of loss

And a struggle to survive and follow a boss

But to be real, present and fair

If these ideals were simple, they would involve no dare

For if a man is to rise from his roots in the dark

These are some of the truths to mark

To run from anything that is strange and new

May indeed be a reflex that's saved more than a few

But without the curiosity, to shed some light

On what is not known, would leave us to live in perpetual night

So if anything can change the course of what's to come

It's not more of the past, violence and a gun

But rather to pick up where a wrong turn was taken

It's long overdue we were made to awaken.

CONVERSATION

May 2017

Have you ever considered the content of your talk?

Does curiosity lead you to explore important things or just balk?

When opinions start to diverge

Do you not feel an unmistakable urge

You start to sense how this might turn

Time to move on and avoid the burn

Here in the city, conflict arises every day

Little attention to each other do we pay

And have you noticed, if someone wrongs you, however slight

If you speak up, no apology will you get, just a fight

I find it striking how things have changed

The rules of courtesy have become rather strange

Others might say they no longer exist

But let's go with the thought, and unclench that fist

Many years ago, before I left

True we were fewer, though there was much theft

And violence hung like a fog that wouldn't leave

It wasn't much fun to watch people question what to believe

Security or tolerance. They shouldn't cancel out

That they did at that time, there was little doubt

But one thing seemed to remain

Amidst all of the strife, the tension, the pain

When waiting for the bus, on line

People behaved, and everyone was fine

I would cite this example while overseas

When Europeans would step on each other like hungry bees

Yet on my return I was stunned to note

Taking others into consideration no longer did float

And conversation, the thoughts we exchange

Facilitated now by these smart phones that derange

An interface has crept between humans with a need to talk

At times, I'll admit I've listened, but at what I heard I had to balk

So many words to say nothing of any import

It seemed to me like prisoners shouting to each other, each locked in a fort

Unable to bridge whatever separated these ardent technology users

The less they connected, the more they talked – abusers

Unaware of their surroundings, caring even less

The very existence of others was just part of the mess

Step over, ignore, push or shove

Clearly not the home of brotherly love

Things have gone so far, cognition has suffered

Our feelings for others have been seriously buffered

Numbed, one might say, to the point they no longer exist

All that matters are my messages, my apps and my contact list

Now one could accept this as technologies faul

For argument's sake, over any disagreement let's vault

But the infection has taken a new form

And altered the social interaction norm

When two people talk, the purpose is no longer the same

After greeting each other with their appropriate names

One picks a subject and starts to speak

And speak, and speak, and speak, and speak

What matter if the other listens or is bored

Since it's all about me, any information exchanged can be stored

But it won't be as the other feigns interest, making believe

Smiling, nodding, waiting for an opening to leave

Unless, of course, they've not noticed what was about

Lost in their own thoughts, why does this person have to shout

Should I just but in, by now it's my turn

Fortunately, I can block out the noise so my brain doesn't burn

Oh well, I'll just look at my watch and check the time

Say "I'd love to talk more, but I've got to get to the Apple Store and stand in line"

Everyone knows that's code for I'm cool and rushed

And I'll have to see about having those photos airbrushed

So what has transpired between two members of evolution's crown jewel?

It seems to me we've evolved into a species of fools

Spoken language, that single thing that gave birth to civilization

Is no longer used to feed the intellect of out nation

Words, the tools that allow us to think

And transcribed into books, of paper and ink

Now function like electrons, just a constant flow

And after the talk, what did we learn, and what do I know?

THE TALK

July 2017

To always avoid discussing what must be discussed

Forms a coating on relationships, something like rust

To live always now in the present tense

May at first seem like very effective defence

Have you wondered though, defending against who

Let's go on as if you knew

 talk is to bridge the distance separating us all

We claim connection is our goal, overall

Yet it seems to me we've labored in the other direction

Which is why everyone seems to be starved for affection

For this distance we speak of, a place of intimacy

Seems to have become for most, quite scarey

So instead of bringing us closer indeed

Conversation now serves the wary, in word and deed

Even when two people are living together

Tensions occur, spoiling the weather

For to raise an issue risks rocking the boat

And in so doing, whatever keeps it afloat

Prudence when dealing with matters explosive

It's advice often heard, though why does one give?

Counsel that allows the infection to endure

Though in the moment it probably seems more sure

And reasons there are, for people all have limits

To how much "truth" they can hear – hours or minutes

For these truths drill down to the insecurities ignored

And the resentments accumulated so carefully stored

Open the door to let one demon out

But as they are too numerous, you'd better watch out

For once opened this door, it's impossible to close

Anyone who has tried it surely knows

Though we all talk of communication, honesty and trust

There can be no question, in any relationship it's a must

That to be real one must build it slowly, over time

And carefully nurtured, like some fine wine

To be opened with care, given time to breathe

So it can adjust to the atmosphere, immediate tensions relieve

Sadly, we all seem to do follow the first course

Why take a risk? Bet on the safer horse

So this trust, this wine, so essential for truths to reveal

That the inevitable wound can be cleaned and heal

Shaken or shocked, the wine will turn

Vinegar not fine wine, will you find in the urn.

Turning back to the "talk" every couple knows

On the outside it's usually wrapped in fine paper and bow

That must be removed at great risk and much care

Courage, my friends, when accepting the dare

If the foundation was solid and well maintained

And the trust and love practiced, its reason to be was retained

Any bump in the road can be overcome

Is that not the purpose of such a bond, it's true sum?

But for those who choose to see no elephant in the room

Who prefer rather the external illusion to groom

When the need to talk inevitably comes

And the question arises – butter or guns?

If care was not taken from the very start

Every hurt, so carefully stored in the wounded heart

Will come rushing through, like some tidal wave

And there will little chance of this thing to save

To those who say "you think too much, just move on"

"They'll get over it," or "don't dwell upon"

The choices one makes each and every day

Like bricks of some edifice that you lay

Think you're building something that will impress

The neighborhood, the schools, the right address

One morning you may, unwary awake

And find this building is really a fake

Build it strong from the start, not the easy way out

If trust isn't compounded daily, its place will most likely be ceded to doubt

A well known author, back in the day

Wrote a book called Love and Will – and he had a lot to say

Explaining in terms both erudite, simple, with skill

Put the subject literally through the mill

Love is Eros, the cherub, there to attract

Never meant to endure, he never promised a durable pact

What makes it last, and this may surprise

Is the will to love, how's that for wise?

Passion gives way, as it must after a time

To caring for another's well being is now as important as mine

The promise that's made to both, if made for real

Holding fast to it will see you through life, letting the inevitable wounds to heal

Scars will form, marking how far you have come

And as time marches on you can say to yourself "well done."

THE ESSENTIAL

April 2017

All my life I have sought something true

Something old and eternal, not something new

Why one might ask was a quest such as this?

My path, never questioned. Was I remiss?

In never questioning why my method requires that I always ask why

How is it that I gave myself such a crucial bye?

I guess it seemed natural to assume that all things flowed

To that core, the central place, the eternal light that glowed

But did I miss something along the way?

The events that occur each and every day

Must they be seen through this lens eternal?

Ignoring the daily struggles, the quiet infernal

I notice while conversing with those otherwise preoccupied

It's not always possible to convey why all that has transpired

Goes back to one truth, disqualifying inadvertently

How others might explain just as diligently

I am attentive. I notice how they view

As we discuss events, old and new

My gripe, my complaint for so many years

The questions I ask are all about fears

Why do so many stop at the very first chance?

Instead of pushing onward, to find a place where to take a stance

My explanations at times seem self-serving, even if true

An obstacle is thus constructed, I know, by what I do

No one wants to be shown what they have ignored

How easily they are satisfied, proud, yet bored

For curiosity is its own reward

And in its entirety, must be considered and stored.

The classics, working only with imited tools

Many working today disparage these authors and consider them
fools

But minds that are free from numbers and hands

Can be unrestrained by practicalities' demands

To soar in one's mind across land and sea

To imagine what rules the world and makes us be

To create in thought what exists not yet here

Pure Imagination knows not any fear

Yet when the concrete boundary is crossed

Courage may fail, and much can be lost

Like the winter cold, if descends like a frost

Its sparkle of newness demands a heavy cost

Thus science was born in the head of man

It exists to bridge and make a plan

To challenge, validate, ensure a fact

Its values: rigor, honesty in thought and act

Yet odd how these promising new tools

With their strict guidelines and transparent rules

Have come to play tricks on us as answers we seek

As money gained in importance, our spirits grew weak

In our rush to know more, to be the first

To claim the glory, the fame and quench that thirst

The search became a race, the values deformed

Is it time now for all inquiry to be reformed?

We praise education, the technical skills

The bells and the whistles and all those frills

Have they taken the place of the long journey required?

In the present, the new, somehow we've grown inextricably mired

Those who came before us, who labored and thought

Were less concerned by new technology for none could to be
bought

Their careful observation and unfettered minds

Provided a freedom of now abandoned kinds

Though secure in what we know now

We rather laugh at them than bow

But forgetting how we got from there to here

Deprives us of humility, as we value only what is near

New terms invented to replace what came before

A specialist's language to the layman closes many a door

To the non initiate, not part of the select few

They're stuck in ignorance, what can they do

And we, the inventors of the new

Forget where it came from and how it grew

The dreams of those who came before

Laid the foundation of all that exists and more

Have we exhausted their imaginings, though most were wrong?

Or did the leaps of their minds leave more stanzas to their song?

More important still, one mustn't always look back

But has our reductionist method opened our minds at least a crack

So take a moment to consider how today came to be

Great thinkers from another time further were able to see

Tied to our numbers helps, there can be no doubt

At times it just seems we've grown smaller with more numbers about.

I don't think I'd have had a thoughts such as these

When life was busy and there was not time my curiosity to tease

But now with the luxury of time to think

I've noticed how much of today's Kool Aid we drink

To step back from the demands of the day and actually reflect

To use the greatest tool at our disposal, one that is almost perfect

The one that can span space and time

Without money or machines or data sets to climb

The one that can point in a direction that's new

Can any machine do that? If so, there are but a few.

THE FIXERS

April 2017

There are a group of us, though rarer we grow

I have no statistics but experience has let me know

Who seem to care more than those we meet every day

They tend to ask questions wanting only to hear what others have to say

Who are they and how are they born?

Was it their choice or the world's fabric that's torn?

That such a group as we

Was so needed to be

To join those others of their kind

Of a caring, repairing, seriious mind

It seems the world is today more concerned

With harvesting, hoarding, natural treasures burned

To steward the wonders that were given

Or too the edge of extinction, driven

Existence requires balance to survive

Must so many disappear for other's to thrive?

But could Nature an error possibly have made?

When to only one species she gave a lethal blade

The means to disrupt this shared place

And become the imperfect dominant race

Filled with a hunger that knows no bounds

Capable of hearing none of the warning sounds

Believing that life's limits exist only for those of a lesser kind

For we alone, are endowed with our superior mind

All we need do is to want and then to find

Ignoring by choice how we have grown blind

Yet these are questions far beyond my scope

Why then do only some notice, care and hope?

Is it something from birth, do they have keener eyes?

That see between the lines and beyond the lies

Or were they wounded at an age too young?

Sensitized, to right a wrong, by an experience that stung?

It is not rational, this imperative

To know deep down its more important to give

Some seek others likeminded for courage and strength

Collectively, some will go to any length

Grand gestures they yearn to perform

In the hope of somehow altering the present norm

Others, more singular is their way

Speak out to others each and every day

Pointing out to those living near

The cost of not holding what we were given, dear

Not just that which we claim is ours

Since in the grand scheme of things, it lasts but a few hours

It to see beyond the here and how

And wonder how we can allow

To labor towards our own demise

Explain to me in what way this is wise.

THE GUIDE

June 2017

Of the many voices that seek our choices to guide

Some claim the limelight, others seek to hide

Some come from the world of a shifting tide

But the most important come from inside

To further complicate their identification

They are the many facets dating back to creation

Each a pole, a system unifying all experience, related

Going back to the beginning, before things were dated

With needs and demands to serve their goal

Each striving for inner coherence, to make them whole

Cacophany results for these pieces don't neatly fit

Like atoms randomly colliding, each other they hit

Hidden or lost in the daily din

They move unrecognized ready to sin

From our perspective, the small part of which I'm aware

Too much going on to see what they prepare

And not only that, their reach knows no bounds

They occupy stealthily the entire undergrounds

Somehow working together, nature guiding their way

Yet each has a role and its lines to say

For they are composed of elements or ourselves we've pushed aside

By the rules we live they were thought not able to abide

Since that day, they live in the shadows, shy and defamed

Their guilt never proven, undesirables were they named

Frustration builds as their efforts fail

Only from the darkness can they seek to assail

The neat clean mask in the daylight we wear

We live between daylight and nighttime – one world sees all, the other totally unaware

Has your curiosity been piqued, of whom do I speak?

Is there some force within me, draining me, making me weak?

I can't see it, I can't find it. How do I know that it's real?

Could something inside me my independence steal?

It's an old idea that shook the world

When thrust into our consciousness it was hurled

Into a world that thought human will was the last word

Can one prove that something flies if it's not a bird?

So much of this world exists that we can't see

Though these things can direct our lives undeniably

Then what should one do, believe or deny?

Embrace the possibility or the lie?

Such was the dilemma way back when

The notion of an unconscious emerged from Freud's pen

It shook the world in that time when the will was king

An earthquake erupted with a might sting

For a time interest was high, this thing we must know

If it's there, there must be some way it to show

To touch it, to dissect it, to tear it apart

After all, we'd around that time raised vivisection to a high art

Success was meager, methods only indirect

Vague patterns, unexplainable behaviors were the only way to detect

So given this frustration, a question was asked

Since it can't be studied, with another approach let's be tasked

Let's set this aside and look only at that which we can touch, feel and see

A whole new world of exploration came to be

Only that which can be empirically touched, measured and probed

That way our results would be clear and the truth, finally showed

As science advanced, and means of measurement grew more precise

We started to have data, isn't that nice?

Few seemed to care we'd constructed a tautology

And with it came a new ideology

Though pesky this invisible thing we can't see

It continued, in spite of our efforts at denial, to influence reality

But high minds can be closed minds when challenges go unmet

A decision it seems was made and the paradigm set

Progress of a sort continued, though the denial remained

New discoveries bring us closer, but how much has really been gained?

New cures, new explanations, new avenues of research

Progress is good, far be it from me to besmirch

Yet behind every symptom lies a story untold

And if life is a narrative that continues to unfold

With distance and a fresh eye, many things fall into place

The meaning grows clearer as we follow the trace

I know it's much simpler to explain things in objective terms

Guilt is something unpleasant as once revealed, it burns

In our rush to avoid things we'd rather not see

A question must be asked in all humility

This thing that we'd decided is of little import

This thing one can't study, understand or report

Is ignoring it completely, is dismissal the way?

Do we really believe that if we continue, it will just go away?

So here's a thought not meant to disrupt

Though I'm certain many will protest and find my intervention abrupt

Accept what we can't see, not everything must have material form

Take a fresh look at it, and find a way to bring it back into the norm

Nothing exists that everything by itself can explain

Every element deserves more respect than disdain

For there is no denying, great influence it can claim

So study it on its own terms if our goal is to stay sane.

THE PAST

March 2016

I thought I'd decided to leave behind the past

How many years ago – 10, 20 or maybe just the last

And yet when I think of the progress I've made

The result is clear, those wages were not fully paid

Small changes, sure, superficial in fact

More in thought and word, less so in act

Do we think to will it different;y, is that enough?

To liquidate a balance (or deficit) of experience can be very tough

Patterns are set through repetition in early years

When we learn to be governed most of all by our fears

Not a pretty picture when seen in the harshest light

The driving need, the truth, needs a hero in the fight

Some escape. these beings now smart and free

Why is it then I can't answer the simplest question – who is me?

I know first and best what others have said

Taking their cues, I made my bed

The linens may conform, neat looks the bed

I may lie in it, but something feels strange, foreign, a bit dead

Does this feeling come from what just happened, words that were said?

Have I heard them before, expecting them to be read?

By those whose job it is to protect and teach

How the world works, and how the summits to reach

But if I'm ill-suited, something I must change

Will the disparate parts not the whole derange?

Young though I was, no means to choose

Listen and follow or my way I may lose

For these things I must abandon, are they really all bad?

I wonder at this, for to lose so much of myself makes me sad

Was there perhaps another way?

If only it hadn't had to be sacrificed that day

From one's supposed demons much one can learn

Is the only possible fate for them in hell to burn?

But if sides were taken and our vote went to the others

Did no one speak up for me, even demons deserve mothers?

For is their evil so clear and absolute?

When seen more completely, can they ever be cute?

After all, for reasons one rarely considers or understands

Perhaps their truth was for later, brought forth by other hands

Were they truly evil or requiring of time?

To bring nuance and purpose for them to be mine

A question of timing perhaps – had they but spoken another day

Had their words come out or been heard in some other way

For if they are cast down into my personal cell

Have I not condemned them to a life in my personal hell?

A dark place where they can neither grow nor learn

Of course they'd resent me, even against me turn?

Betrayed, they might labor in darkness, bitter and stern

And denied each day, hotter the fire will burn.

So I lie down wondering if the system I can beat

And what harm might it do if it got too close to the heat?

But what of the sheets I've not chosen, not suiting my décor?

What if their color, their form or their pattern are a bore?

Whose guidance did I follow, was there something essential I chose
to ignore?

At the end of the day I wonder what am I doing and more
importantly, what for?

Each choice affirms something new, we think we need

Unknowingly rejecting its opposite, of which we no longer take
heed

This former friend, once part of our core

Gets shoved into darkness, and we close the door.

It will plot and scheme, laboring in the dark

Its crosshairs focused, you yourself are its mark

So take a fresh look, how best to proceed

Ignore its warning, or fail not to take heed

Irresistible its force, growing stronger the longer denied

Locked up perhaps, but it never died.

For within this darkness life abounds

Long ago it was pushed out of bounds

Condemned, but not dead, frustration grows

Living in a place that no one knows

Abandoned, betrayed, what have we done?

Would it not be more merciful to use a gun?

Misery, like some plants, can grow high and tall

If it gets too high, someone will fall

We'd all regret the loss somewhat reservedly

But was the condemned truly at fault and punished deservedly?

And that's the point, for what lies within

Were these parts of ourselves punished for what wasn't a sin?

At the time it may have seemed the right thing to do

After all, at that age, we believe the others better knew

But if things aren't clicking the way that they should

Perhaps its time to consider if within the" bad" hides some "good"

If change is what you're after, what you need

Lift the shades, let the sun shine in, let your demons feed

For returned to their home, their rightful place

If you watch closely, you'll see subtle changes in their face

More human, more friendly, more normal in a word

Don't we all respond when our true selves are heard?

Stand ready now beside us, to complete our view

Rich from their perspective, life can seem new.

Change you wanted, here it is

Feel the buzz, feel the fizz

It may tingle, tickle and derange some

But just perhaps with your new friends and maybe that race can be won.

THE POWER OF NO

March 15, 2014

There are two choices one can make

Regardless of what's in fact, at stake

When looking to the future, the road ahead

As we rise each day from our slept in bed

We can pull the sheets back to their madel position

Or we can take them off and make a decision

Return to the past, with its discomforts perverse

The unresolved challenges that keep us blocked in reverse

How odd it is, the comfort we find

In this unsatisfactory, conflicted, state of mind

Where the thought of the new, so attractive at first

When all that's left is to cross the line in one final burst

But at the moment, when we are set to gain

From somewhere deep within rises an irresistible pain

We can't attach it to something clear

All we know is its pervasive fear

As nearer we draw and the line grows wide

And we start to look around for some place to hide

From the distance a precipice begins to appear

We start to see the drop as we sense the danger, now clear

The cliffs with itheir edges sharp and rough hewn

Decision time approaches – it's high noon.

The odor of danger surrounds us as we approach

Our courage wanes, fears begin to encroach

Reason fails, emotions seize control

Who cares anymore about becoming whole?

We take a step back and call off the bet

Have we fallen once again into the past's "fear" net?

Why does this happen when all logic is defied?

When the mind plays its games, to ourselves have we once again lied

It is a lie which we know contains no truth

Confined as if trapped inside an old phone booth

Caught in this space restricted, now stuck

Gave up on myself once again – what the fuck?

We can see what transpires in the world outside

Some inner force makes us want to hide

Better to stay safe, immobile, inside

We don't make the rules but should we not by them abide?

Coming back to decision time, the yes or the no

What drives the choice to give up or grow?

Life deals us cards, a hand to play

Our early years plot strategy, to play the game or stray

Rarely is dealt a hand that offers a clear choice

One look at the cards and know we do have a voice

Not all of the cards are bad, regardless their count

There are always a few good ones, up to us to let them amount

To a handle, credible and real

It's a game of chance, of skill, enjoy it, heal

Must I win to live, so black and white

Life isn't binary, so fight the good fight

For as the game evolves and cards are exchanged

What some consider fate or destiny can be deranged

To our strengths or weaknesses we play our hand

That should determine in part where we will land

The best answers most often rraise a question new

What drives one to play poorly, why this would we do?

In this land of bounty and the American dream

Where all is froth, pizza and ice cream

We have focused on that which comes quickly and with ease

Money is the answer, the game, the ultimate tease

Who has time to reflect, to consider or understand?

The choices we make will always determine how we play our hand

And why do we so often come up short?

When in theory all we must do is walk onto the court

Don't overthink this, just too hard to face

To look back in time and recognize the obvious trace

Back to the time when we first learned to play

When the rules were set, and we thought we were here forever to stay

But time is finite, we are given just so much

As it slips through our fingers with nary a touch

Why have things not worked in the way we had planned?

Did we so poorly play our hand?

Or was it was luck, destiny or fate?

Something beyond our control always made us too late

When did it become too hard to assume?

That we built the walls, the windows, the room

Who wrote that what I want is mine for the asking?

Where's that promotion, born to live in the sun, basking

Our role in this, how much we get to decide

Do I enter the fray or from it hide?

Ceding control to others who fate has mistakenly assigned

It is what it is – so say us all, resigned.

Did you ever think the world offer two roads - "I can or I can't"

Complaints, blame others, have you not heard the rant?

We live in two worlds – aware of but one

That's where the trouble starts, with the endless fun

Like seeing with but one eye alone

Or having a telephone with only a microphone

We speak all the time, forgetting we must also hear

Ignoring the warnings as the danger grows ever more near

Talk louder we do since that's all that we know

Distraction our salvation as more seeds of destruction we sow

new religion is thus born, a faith in mindless noise

We fill our lives with entertainment and high tech toys

But life can't be ignored, it follows its logical way

As we misplay our cards each and every day

So that even our good cards are mistakenly tossed

As more and more hands come to be lost

Failure digs a hole deep and profound

Like a pit extending well below the ground

And as we sink, the walls higher do grow

Until our new prison has become our home and all that we know

Darkness now comes from within

Are we cursed, though unable to recall a particular sin

Cursing our birth, what is the way out?

Complaining has turned courage into a pout

And so it goes, deeper each day

Until our confidence has left us, afraid to enter any fray

Life can be generous if we welcome her call

It's not reserved for the few, but for us all

The difference resides in a simple fact

When she calls, what do we say, how do we act?

If one responds present, again she will call

If absent, she'll feel no welcome, only a wall

For there is power in the words that we say

And the chance to use them happens each day

My reward may not come as I wished it to be

But at least a way forward I now clearly see

In life there is no and there is yes

On how we answer will come the more or the less

An old God in resurgence, his message vague and unclear

He preaches doubt, mistrust and fear

His Gospel explains failure as fate

Best to embrace it sooner rather than late

Take no chances, lose one's hope

That's the best way with life to cope

Take nothing seriously, life's a bad joke

Play to lose, truly go for broke

And so the power of No has arrived

It has been around forever and has always survived

Its practice expands, gaining new acolytes each day

You can see it happen, when you hear many words spoken with little to say

Silence this noise, look within

Learn to listen, focus, block out the din

No promise of success – the undefined

Is less a matter of fact than of mind

To live is to play as best we can

Find values and reasons to live – be a man.

THE QUEST

February 27, 2017

I've been on a quest for too many years

The passage of time has allayed my fears

As who I am now standing on firmer ground

Yet what I search for remains unfound

My eyes have been open, more clearly I see

Having acquitted myself of my obligations, I am now free

I know what's important, having put in the time

The values that guide me are truly mine

Now the externals are there too, I believe that's clear

I look like the right package, so others should draw near

Small talk comes easily, with a note of personal concern

Humor warms things up without heating up to a burn

A nice place to live, financially secure

Athletic. Intelligent. Caring. Fun – For sure.

There is one obvious downside, I've come to know

It's was unexpected as I've always believed it was our mission to grow

To observe, to listen, to have an open curious mind

One's truth, on this path, one would surely find

This assumes, however, only part of the equation

For we live in the concrete present, part of a nation

And this place we inhabit in a moment in time

Has values as well – though ignored – and they are not mine

Were the years away, learning new things abroad

They shed a different light revealing much that was flawed

Now differences abound, one must take note

Some are better here, others there – no cause to gloat

It's like having two eyes instead of just one

Living only on the surface, certain things may look like fun

But scratch the surface, shine a different light

Suddenly is revealed a disturbing sight

Assumptions abound, though rarely critiqued

If too closely examined, a truth might be leaked

So continue down this path, seeing but with one eye

The world starts to go flat, and we stop asking why

When that happens, ignorance takes hold

We cling to those truths, however old

Can one really believe in dogma, yet call it truth?

Safe from examination, they remain untouchable, aloof

The founding fathers, products themselves of another time

Gave us a gift, a system, benevolent – for most – safe and benign

More than 200 years have come and gone since then

Change has transformed us from way back when

The laws grew to reflect what was new

Many benefitted, not just a few

But now we seem to have come to a time when doubt took hold

Without noticing the change in ourselves, somehow we too have
grown old

No taste for the future, and things unknown

We cling to what we have, fearful of the strong wind that has blown

Look around. We don't recognize how our world has changed

Frightened we've grown angry, deranged

No question, the new, if it comes too fast

Foundations are shaken, we wonder if what we had can it last?

We've got so much, who wouldn't hold tight

Why give it away, let's bicker and fight

Funny how wealth brings greed when the opposite it should be

After all, if there's more than enough, we can share the plenty

And what of time, for a future awaits

Have we prepared for the unknown, or decided only to close the gates

The angry words one hears, clamoring for those days when things were supposedly good

When everyone looked like us in the neighborhood

The economy grew, there was money in the bank with more on the way

We removed ourselves from time, leting others work all day

That job is beneath us, so we'll just pay

And maybe let them stay

It worked for awhile and our minds grew lazy

Thinking only of gratified desires as reason grew hazy

No plan, no vision, no passion no longer abound

Without them, I find little hope anywhere to be found

Only fear, vague, yet everywhere

Protect ourselves only, for others have no care

Infected we became, in our minds and our hearts

We stopped living freely – might as well play darts

Marking our time, no purpose to fulfill

Except paying off the credit card and the electricity bill

And what about those taxes, the government takes from me

Have you ever heard anyone say they didn't work hard – not me?

And give it to those undeserving lazy hordes polluting our shore

If we continue down this path, nothing good lies in store

I could go on, but you surely get the gist

Do we open our hand, or clench a fist?

Neither, it seems, would the pragmatist say

We sink or we swim together, so everyone must pay

The strong help the weak, the rich the poor

The smart can teach, the wise ensure

But where are these people, do they care?

Though some say present, most don't dare

They've made it, so now their goal is clear

There is only one thing they must fear

That the government comes to take for that's what they do

And these poor rich folks, though they be very few

Will have to do with less, their ascendant is stopped

The castle walls must come down and the drawbridge dropped

It's time to awake from this fantasy which has mislead us so

Let the sun rise up and realize what we forget we need to know

The stories, the myths we create to reassure and validate

Do they not betray who we are if their foundations reside in hate

If that which separates us is unknowingly what we seek

If there's room in our perfect system only for the strong and not the weak

If the competition we praise as the savior, all knowing and fair

Did it not cost us something precious – how to care?

Not just for ourselves, but for one another

We all are the same in some way mother, father, sister and brother

And the success of one resides on a nation built by many

Without this cohesive body, there would be no nation, not any

So next time you feel your anger mounting – justified though it might be

Pause for a moment, and ask yourself if you've considered all that you see

Or was your vision limited to that one eye

The one that wants the whole, entire pie

f course we can't just take if and give it away

But that's a discussion to be had by us all one day

And decide, this time thinking and feeling, who we want to be

What kind of future could we have, if only we could see

We've been walking these many years with eyes glued to the ground

Is there peace, happiness, and a hopeful future – is that what we've found?

When on the wrong path, courage is required

If we sense we are stuck, our feet in the mud are mired

If our spirits grow dark, our hearts cold and alone

It's time to react before we turn to stone

Dare to dream – not of money but discovery

That would be the beginning of our national recovery.

The other, the one who sees and understands

To share a life together, one must have one foot in each other's lands

I've said it before and I'll say it again

Something we've known from way back when

We sink or we swim together, there is no choice

So together again, say yes in one voice.

TIME

May 2017

Time is all we have while here

We think little of it until the end is near

If you are here and for real

Not to only to shop but also to feel

If you have learned by now who you are

If you have found your true north star

If you know how you have come so far

And if you've always place high the bar

If you don't need yet another pair of shoes

If you believe you have fairly paid your dues

And have no time to sing the blues

Then prepare yourself for some very good news

You are rich in a way that needs no money

Knowing life's sweetness can be warm and sunny

With a firm belief that each day could be funny

With someone sleeping beside you that you call honey

Wise to the point your heart follows no fad

With Juliet who said the more she gave the more she had

Goodness inhabits you spirit not bad

Though life is a challenge you are not sad

An adventure now awaits

No key is required to open the gates

Fear not. Dare to Challenge the fates.

And not to worry over broken plates

You've made your journey and learned much on the way

When you speak it's to learn or to play

Curiosity has nourished your soul

Filling in the blanks and made you whole

Living life in this manner is its own reward

Life is a train – welcome aboard

Be wise, not fearful, your treasures don't hoard

They'll weigh you down, worry will make you bored

If in these strange couplets something resonates

If you feel you've been smiled on by the fates

If another adventure you believe awaits

Then perhaps we do share many of the same traits.

TO GIVE

April 2017

Some of us are born to give

Indeed we must for us to live

For purpose drives our direction

We find no reason in life's discretion

To seek only appetites gratified

To live but to be desired

To taste life's pleasures for ourselves alone

Why? No greater sin exists to atone

Now the question arises, how many is the count?

Are they numerous or but a small amount?

And what of balance, has Live thought of that?

Or would that be a solution far too pat?

My own experience – anecdotal at best

Provides no answer that can meet the test

But I can say in no uncertain terms

Since experience is the source of all one learns

In this time, in this place

Where our kind don't live, they race

The other – not to mention a "Thou"

No time is allotted to allow

Before I came to realize

Before I'd grown to be somewhat wise

It urked me, for it always seemed

Where was the one of whom we all have dreamed

The one who would care to know not just my name

And how much they could enjoy from whatever my fame

Childish, of course, for we are not made this way

Somehow Copernicus had not yet spoken his human say

The sun, it seems revolves around us

Divine authorities declared it thus

Shocking when forced to accept

We were not the center of all God kept

Was it always like this in every land?

Was no one born wanting to extend a hand?

To cure, to heal, to shepherd creation

As if, like some god, we could avoid anhillation

Consuming all they lay in our sight

And more than willing to die and fight

To preserve what belonged to none in name

It was given to us all, like praise and blame

Our world is finite, it begins and ends

We plant and harvest, bounty Nature sends

We mine and fish and hunt and kill

Is this generosity ever to be repaid, is there no bill?

A strange thought perhaps for in my time it won't come due

So why should I worry, why should I stew?

But isn't that just the point?

When, divine, ourselves did we anoint?

Blinded by our hungers, yet with bellies full

We rage through this world like some crazed bull

Admiring all we've built, yet blind to what was lost

Who cares really if someone else pays the cost?

They say politics is local, so I see only what is mine

If next door things don't' go so well, for me, that's fine

But there is but one world, not two

If we don't learn to accept this, there will remain of us very few

Not to mention the creatures large and small

Whether they walk, run, swim, fly or crawl

And Nature's bounty which provides for us all

What if that machine is caused to stall?

So on this Earth Day 2017

Though here it's raining and the sky looks mean

Pause for a moment, and ask the question

And perhaps it might cause a serious indigestion

Let's hope this happens, the clock is ticking

If not, we're primed for a major licking.

There will be no winners, all will lose

It's really only up to us, not our leaders, to choose

TWO MINDS AT WAR

Chris/Hank Series

June 2017

We've known each other for the past few years

I've watched you struggle, even shed some tears

Trust you say has abandoned your heart

And so you live alone and apart

A young man in search of a home

Pursued by twin forces with many sins to atone

One is good, keeping him alive with a promise of some hope

One is dark, his protector, standing guard, allowing him to cope

One shows glimmers of things he could do

One sees threats everywhere, blocking every road new

One holds the reins for a few days at a time

One recedes until he gets too close, the ultimate crime

Back and forth in an endless round

I wonder how he lives, of body and mind sound

Not completely, of course, for no real progress can be made

His life crumbles slowly, and he is always afraid

How to break this mortal cycle

Like that old theory of the bicycle

As long as you are moving, you will not fall

But stop for a moment and you will lose all

No peaceful nights, always on the move

Every new chance sabotaged, that's his grove

I've tried so many times to pull him from the storm

To let go of this torment into which he was born

But it's now too late, this is who he's become

To give it up, to change – impossible - the dark side has won

I fought against the darkness, and there were times when I thought

A chance at a better future, with my help he had bought

We could get so close to crossing that line

But as the walls started to shake, darkness said "no, you are mine,:

This last time of many when I'd promised to stop

How to abandon someone with such promise and leave him to a future with mop?

For if he survives, in question, every day

That's about all he'll manage to find to earn his pay

In a few years, after he's beaten down

I see not a man but the remnants of a clown

What I fear most for him, though inevitable it seems

In this land of labels and pills that kills all dreams

Bipolar, perhaps if that reassures some doctor's soul

He'll be stable, medicated, yet fallen into a deeper hole

One from which but a few manage again to be free

But living as he does, that's not in his future what I see

Institutionalized, placed under the state's care

A specialist, a custodian, whose mission is really only to be there

To stick a label on a chart, then medicate

And that's where it ends, numbed, hazy, prepared only to wait

Wait for what? What's the outcome? Where does this lead?

Nowhere really, though they will see to every practical need

And what of those who brought him into this world so rough

To never care for him, concerned with other stuff

He was his mothers insurance his father would marry

But he was not one to linger or tarry

No hand to guide him, no heart to care

They left him, rejected, with a cold stare

For they set him on a path of who he was to become

If they cared any less,, they'd have provided a gun.

His road to salvation dissolving as we speak

He must always be strong and never weak

Each day a reminder his life would have no Sun

Yet he pushes on knowing his future – he has none

So this last time when it looked as if it was finally the one

When he'd no longer sleep in the subway, but awake in the sun

The games he would play with himself, each side there to win

One hiding an object and calling it out as the other's sin

Only to "find" it after a time has passed

A game called "kill trust," for me this time was to be the last

How can a mind remain whole when torn in two?

When each in mortal combat every day they renew

Perhaps it's lasted so long is become a way of life

If things are peaceful, he sheathes his knife

Living on the run, but running from who?

One side chases the other, it's a habit now, so he knows what to do

But to live otherwise, to stop the train

No longer can I help him, however I explain

Some external force, if life can be kind

Will break the cycle that's captured his mind

Or if God's anger has leftovers from the day he was born

Then from the tissue of life it will end, from its fabric he'll be torn

No peace this scenario brings to me

I could have been a father to him, teach him how a man to be

When one loses a child – be it one's own or that of another

There's no easy how, the sense of waste, to smother

So I try to recall both sides of this young man

And hope against hope he will find another fan

When the time is right and Life finally ends the round

And he can stop running - that God may allow him to be safe and be found.

2 SISTERS

July 2015 – June 2017

I started this when the girls first were married. There was a difficult period between them when a distance installed itself. I watch over them always, ready to intervene in my role once removed. Writing this two years ago, I hit a brick wall, and couldn't finish it. By chance, on this eve of Father's Day 2017, I found it again, and to my great surprise, it finished itself.

I remember the days you both arrived in my life

Caught up in the excitement, there to help my wife

Each one, an event I recall still

How with that mix of emotions my heart did fill

Reassured that you were healthy and strong

And how my life had changed, no longer to me alone did it belong

For now I was bigger than I'd ever been before

No matter what happened, with my life I would guard the door

Thoughts turned next to the future they might find

And with it a blessing that health, love and safety, to you Life would be kind

As each day passed, lost in every mundane event

Feedings, diapers, little sleep, work – paying the rent

The tapestry began, each knot attaching your soul

So you would know where you began on your path to becoming whole

That was my wish, a Father's task

To provide the answers so you would never need to ask

And now that you're grown, with lives busy and full

A new question emerges, demanding from my bag of experience, a new answer I must pull

Two sisters, we assume, if raised together for years

Would they not always reach for each other, in smiles and tears?

It's so easy to forget the complex mix from which they came

Mother and Father, forgetting their differences, bearing one name

But that cannot last, nor would it be good

For a bond to be strong, one cannot mix steel and wood

Families, we imagine, are the unshakeable foundation

They come first and serve to unite in one single nation

But nations are diverse, and politics are played

Allies are sought, compromises are made

All this happens slowly, each plays its part

And the reasons that motivate are different for each and every heart

Some see the larger purpose, to build a stronger cart

Others are self-serving, with designs to tear things apart

Unknowing children bathe in this conflicted water

No matter if boy, girl, son or daughter

Each child, an emergent, unfinished blend

Their own garden, early on, they start to tend

Part mother, part father, but mostly their own

Such is the ground that in each seed is sown

Families are ties made of body and blood

Irrational, neurotic, more emotion than reason, young minds they flood

Interpret – rightly or wrongly – what they see

Sides are taken, the devil's mix, none are free

The task these first score years, school, friends, ambition

Are the scrolls on which these stories are written

They exist perhaps, but are never seen

Their hand firmly on the pen, not fully understanding what their words mean

Problems arise, seemingly with no rhyme or reason

Why don't things work according to the season?

She who had little idea of why she did what she did

Her true self never found, so behind masks she hid

Two girls with only a female phantom as guide

It must have been hard for them with no mother who ever really tried

For like a boy learns from his father how to be a man

Little girls need more than dolls and dresses in life to take a stand

Though the values they find as they grow and learn

Everyone needs a north star telling them when to turn

So though all seemed well on the surface of things

Pretty rooms, birthday parties, dresses and rings

No guiding light was there to point the way

Harder for girls who too often still watch what they say

So each with her strengths and flaws

Trying to understand the world and its laws

The elder, granted beauty as an early gift

Discovered her mother's jealousy, and found a deep rift

Instead of rejoicing in what nature had given her child

Instead of peace, joy, even pride so mild

The adulation thus bestowed burned mother to the quick

Why not me, mother asked, did nature not pick?

Funny how children sense the truth on their own

Though unaware they recognize the rift has grown

Conflicts arise, rivalries too

Characters emerge from this simmering brew

"I will not yield" though mother you may be

"I am prettier than you – all the world this can see"

So a war began, lasting still to this day

Preferring the heat of resentment to having clearly their say

To resolve these old conflicts that tarnish one's sense of self

Vindication more important than peaceful coexistence and wealth.

The conflict takes on a life of its own

The true reasons denied, not to be spoken or known

Distances that should be fluid solidify

And the truth dissolves into a lie

The younger one, living first in her sister's realm

Contented herself to follow, leaving to others the helm

But that was not to be forever, she had a mind of her own

It just took a bit longer for it to be known

An adolescence darkened by forces still ignored

Sailing through school – perhaps she was bored

To this day, so she says, she can't explain why

Marley and Morrison ruled, only dark clothes would she buy

In time, she came into her own

In so many ways she had blossomed and grown

But the darkness was not queried to know its reason

And so it has lasted more than a season

Perhaps the conflict brewing between father and mother

The differences grew creating almost another

A third member of the couple that should have been but two

Whose sole purpose was the sharpen the divergences – though at the time, who knew?

Father at work, getting on with his role

And on the side, with always an eye to his future and becoming whole

Mother, for reasons which she brought from her past

Her only solution was to nourish her resentment; the dye thus cast

Speak ill of each other, the spouses too often indulged

Though what was truly said, only Father divulged

Mother retreated to the fantasy world from which she came

She was never really ready to join in her husband's name

And so the girls started to take sides

Natural, I guess, but harmony it derides

One embraced conviction, determined to succeed

One remained caught, neutral, uncertain – in spite of all she achieved

As each assumed her life, one here, one over there

One operating in openness, one managed her secrets with great care

For the Father that I was and continue to be

This has been a challenge in the absence of our family

But Life takes charge, as each plots their course

Both, on the surface, embraced the divorce

But scars remain as I watch from afar

It's up to them now to drive their own car

Not everything can be assigned to what came before

And even if it could, each child chooses just how much more

Of life to claim, discovering their desires

As each tends their individual fires

There are times when incomprehension seizes control

The arrival of husbands also took its toll

Though every day when they were young

The same song to them was always sung

I spoke of a sister who never welcomed my coming

Her influence was negative, unpleasant and numbing

I cut her off, no longer in my life to belong

This should not happen in families, it is wrong

So I told my children but for their siste,r they were alone

No one else can accompany them wherever they roam

If trouble should strike, she's the one person you could always phone

It's worth the trouble to ensure that with unbreakable thread the blanket is sewn.

So close when young, how I wish it could endure

To see my children have it – so real, so pure

When it left my life before I arrived

Much was missing, but determined, I thrived

And so it will be for my beautiful girls

One may like beads, the other pearls

Not really, just a metaphor for the differences that rule

I ask only that Life keep them close, kind to each other, and never cruel.

ALONE IS NOT NECESSARILY THE SAME THING AS LONELY

"Loneliness does not come from having no people around, but from being unable to communicate the things that seem important to oneself...."

C.G. Jung

UNDER THE ROCK

October 2016

Under the rock lives all that we've lost

What others have frowned upon, exacting a cost

Bits and pieces of ourselves were banished from sight

To live out their days in perpetual night

They see no reason for this treatment, what did they do?

And was it really wrong? They never knew

Toiling aimlessly, each day with no meaning

Except one – to grow darker and, with anger, seething

The confines of the mind obey no physical laws

No concrete walls, forbidding with awe

And so it grows, this anger without obvious reason

Preparing the moment for the well deserved treason

For if we excise some part of our whole

Reject it from any purpose in our lives, without any role

Like any substance organic that lives in the dark

Rotten, primeaval, fetid and stark

Or so we believe, thusly justifying the choice

But what if we were wrong, and these unwanted pieces were given a voice?

One we could hear, perhaps understand, even redress, the wrong

From a scream might emerge a most precious song

Out of the darkness, creativity is born

It flows freely if we listen, given not torn

For what appears dark is often seen through a lens

Misshaping perception, with twists and bends

But this lens serves masters who see the many, but never the one

It has children but no daughter, nor any son

And parents, those guardians of what's most precious of all

Whose voice do they hear, to whom do they answer when comes the call?

So plon ahead children do, heeding harsh words

Never free to fly the skies like the soaring birds

And to ensure earthbound they will always remain

Told not to ponder the past, it's a silly stain

But the past is the road we followed from there to here

If not understood, how can one's vision be clear?

A bandaid, a pill, self-esteem and more

Splitting hairs won't change what happened – what a bore

Get on with it, have fun, even sex – the pleasures the present offers

Forget about your soul – just be sure to fill those empty coffers

Avidity – the hunger that is never quenched

That tightness around our heart sthat can't be unclenched

The more we devour, though more bland grows the taste

Soon filled with nothing, what a waste

Are we lost, is life empty, no meaning to be found?

Has our ship never left port? Has it run aground?

Where can one look as the waters rise?

Have we always knocked on the same door? Was that wise?

Seized by confusion, where can one turn?

Like the wick on a burning candle, how much time is left to burn?

A door we seek, but which one offers some hope?

Old habits, dear friends, hold fast to the rope

And what of those demons cast off long ago

Were they truly so bad? We don't really know

Do they still live in darkness, under the rock

To think of them scares us. Don't open the lock

Most don't, they stay safe in their emptiness bland

They've abandoned the journey to stay safely on land

But a few have dared to let some daylight in

Will they be punished if to do so means committing a sin?

Yet in the light of day, demons they no longer appear

What made them frightful was our own fear

Fear of what? They were bad and banished for good cause

But seeing them now, in our stomach one question gnaws

The more sunlight that warms under the rock

With each passing tick comes the tock of the clock

The sun warms and it heals, drying out the rot

We wonder, can we talk to these demons? Why not?

They look, in fact, a bit like us

Was it the right decision to throw them under the bus?

I've noticed the more acquainted we grow

Things start to change, wondering what made it so

And then it hits, so clear to see

These demons are really a part of me

One that was mistakenly forced out of its home

It existedfor a reason, only wanting to be known

For these pieces contain elements of all that might be

And the fuel for the fires of creativity

Funny how parents push only the good on their kids

Believing perfection a desirable goal, they seal tight the lids

When, in fact, it's the edgier part

That which will upset the apple cart

The tension created between these two

Provides not only the raw materials, but the heat for the strew

As opposites blend, new forms emerge

As if from deep, dark, primal urge

It's not about adding one thing to a second

Its more about the two confronting while the heat beckoned

Something entirely new now comes in being

Life is enriched by new answers. How freeing!

UNKNOWN LANDS

January 2017

For too many years I've been looking for the one

The other who would seek much more than just fun

Who wanted for themselves to open their hearts

To grow in parallel, yet each owning their separate parts

Can two become one, is that a valid goal?

Or to be one, must each not remain separate, that way become whole

Gaps we have in our lives that we need to complete

The other is not there to accomplish for us such a feat

I see no option, it's a lifetime quest

To follow this path, accepting each test

Solitary must it be, every road leads to some different place

Or is there a convergence, a joining, some grace?

Is this the ground where all roots entwine?

A place to pause, or one to truly call mine?

As I've traveled my road, becoming more my own

Where I look to others for perspective, so myself by myself to be
better known

To be seen through the eyes of another, accepting yet aware

Their regard constant, caring, and fair

With no axe to grind, no need replacing desire

Where caring, not hunger, nourishes the fire

If indeed we are creatures of the earth, elemental, at times even
vile

And the ideals we've created and placed in some master file

As if they were the equal of our deeper nature, so dark

Is there no reward, no paradisiac park?

I've followed this path as best I could

I think in balance I've done less harm, more good

Then why are there times when it seems a dead end?

Looking ahead, the road does not appear to bend

It seems to continue, linear, as the losses grow

I bear them better now, this I know

But the quest inhabits me, something pushes me ahead

Why then when the door opens, only my disappointment is fed?

Why continue down this path to nowhere, or so it seems?

Is what I am searching only the stuff of dreams?

No answer greets me, not even a clue

Just more repetition, nothing truly new

Though this I have learned of late, obvious to see

I've learned what I could from it, yet it won't let me be

Am I caught in some current, confused, even lost?

My moorings broken, was that the cost?

No new rule, no new stars, no prophets appear

Tossed by the waves, going nowhere, yet oddly without fear

Am I crossing the desert, has the order been overthrown?

Leaving behind the familiar, to enter the unknown

But if unknown it be, how will I know?

When do I reach land, and start again to sow?

And to sow what, what might I need?

I've wasted so much time, spilled so much seed

And if this place exists not outside of my mind

If that's the reason I find people selfish and unkind

Unwittingly some kind of God have I become?

If that's the case, it's really no fun.

I leave to Him this role divine

And pick up my own in double time

A God is a God through the power He can wield

I have none of that order, so that place I gladly yield

Now, Lord, it's time – how about that moment of grace?

I need a rest or some inspiration to continue the race

Hope returns for a reason, like the seasons in their regularity

With their own special order, and their diversity

Each one must die so the next can be - Is that not the source of fertility?

Ensuring however it will last for eternity

So weather the storm, wait for the Spring

As long as I move forward, there will be some new thing

The sterile present, though it may sting

I'm alive and kicking, even if not yet ready to sing

WHAT DO YOU SEE?

May 2017

Who am I, why at times, a stranger do I feel?

Somehow not believing the same things are real

As those who inhabit the same place

After all, we share the same space

Humans, our species, the time is now

Why are things so fluid, and we got here how?

On the surface, laughter, conversations abound

And busyness, the new religion, is everywhere to be found

Is this time different from those that came before?

In looking back to the past can one predict what lies in store

For now, we care little, or so it seems

For things like rigor, reflection, and classical means

An odd term, classical, it seems an irrelevant past to evoke

Useless attempts to know from the past, now worthless and broke?

Better to start from a just few years ago

When "real" knowledge began and our data sets began to grow

For pure thought has lost its prior appeal

To have values nowadays, to be considered and real

Correlations, percentages, numbers in limitless amounts

If it can't be quantified (with tables, charts and graphs) it hardly counts

Since those who came before had no numbers to crunch

Clearly their thoughts were wrong, they were out to lunch

So let's rename something in pseudo speak

Just like in the old days with Latin and Greek

It sounds much better, and makes one look smart

And to promote one's work, it looks more real than photoshop art

Whittle it down to a headline or presentation

We now reside in the "Bullet Point Nation"

I offer an example, Autism, that bane of every parents nightmare

Has become epidemic causing tremors of care

What is the cause and how can we treat?

A cause or a cure - either would be great – something clean and neat

If all we can do is observe and describe

With no sure treatment or cure to prescribe

Best we change the name into something savant to reassure

That way reimbursement and funding for research we'll ensure

For have we learned anything really new

Do we know better really what to do?

Or have we simply dressed up the pig?

And ensured for ourselves a long term gig

A spectrum disorder – now there's something new

A brilliant marketing concept – many thanks to the few

Who dreamed up this nebulous concept instead of some finding that informs

So these children who live outside of all norms

Can be truly helped to find a path in life and fit in

And not be considered (in secret) like the fruit of some sin.

To my mind, a disservice has been rendered

And in giving up real thought for numbers, have we something of value surrendered?

WHEN BAD THINGS ARE DONE

April 2017

Did you ever think about the consequences when bad things are done?

What happens to the world at large, when someone gets hurt – and not just one

There is balance in the universe, for if one side should win

The whole thing would be altered, whatever the sin

So when someone gives in to their evil side

Someone else must do good, by this universal law we abide

Does this seem too simple, a child's view of the dark?

Or is it so obvious we miss it's meaning, like some random dog's bark?

A light goes out when evil prevails

When good is done, the wind fills our sails.

Without that light, things look darker and bleak

The strong lose conviction, stronger grow the weak

The dual nature of things is how we were meant to see

It's how we were made and intended to be

For it provides a choice, clear as night and day

We look, we reflect, we choose, then we say

For just as surely as day is paired with light

The darkness leads inexorably into the night

The land is dry, the oceans are wet

It's by our choices our course do we set

Dispense with the excuses, the spin, the lies

We were given the gift of vision, let's use our eyes

For choices can be complex, difficult to make

Taking sides can engage everything, so much at stake

But these are most often creations of our own

Bad choices from the past, like weeds, have grown

Clearly mistakes are part of the game as well

Life can be tolerant so we can learn to tell

What we are made of and why wrong we may do

It's the oldest lesson, by far not the most new

Courses can be changed, once we've found our North Star

What determines the future comes from very near, not far

he truth resides within, if only we look

Clear as the printed page in any children's book

Evil exists, rooted in the mud from which we came

Survival, competition, savagerie, all live under its name

Somehow someone so long ago

Looked up at the sky and needed to know

Is there not a better way that we can admire?

To guide us to a better place, to live and aspire

That's how Good came to be

It's not a given but in general we can see

And know the difference if we dare

All it takes is a bit of care

So that is the equation we need consider

It's not a game of chance. open to any bidder

But a choice, to think larger than just me

To use all our senses and our minds to see

To look backward in time to conjure what might lie ahead

And to choose the light, or darkness, and live in hope, or dread

"Neurosis is always a substitute for legitimate suffering"

C.G. Jung

A term we don't often use anymore, however accuratate and descriptive it may be. Replaced, perhaps, by a more "medical' or "scientific" term, though surely less informative. But the message remains as relevant today as it ever was. Words have qualitative, not quantitative meanings. We should treat them with the respect they deserve for they are the tools of our thought.

TWO LADIES

July 2017

Walking my dogs in Central Park

Early In the morning when it's still dark

One never knows who one might meet

Easier in the park than on the street

The sun comes up and brightens the morn

Many strollers one sees, from their sleep harshly torn

I sit on my rock, where I go every day

A creature of habit, it's just my way

From over the hill, one day months ago

I noticed two ladies surrounded by a glow

It wasn't supernatural, it was more real than that

I wondered if they'd stop to chat

Trailing behind were an odd collection of hounds

Most had been recovered in different pounds

Of ages divers, and sizes too

Indeed, something of a motley crew

I noticed the ladies were each carrying bag

Stopping to pick up trash – a drag

I knew they weren't employees, how could they be

This was their Park, their civic duty they did see

To pick up where others, thoughtless and mean

Simply stepped over what others had discarded as if not seen

I stopped them to ask them what this was about

They looked at me with such a welcome, I knew they were special – without a doubt

We started to speak, of the subject I have no recall

But I knew from that moment these ladies didn't hide behind some wall

The warmth they spread around them, the peace that they brought

Was so real, so natural – it could never be faked, artificial or bought

And so began a daily routine

I look for them each morning, eager and keen

Though all Upper East Side ladies they may be

Of a very special type – so clear to see

One, an artist, a grandmother to fifteen, I think

She builds monumental steel sculptures – why not, some are pink

When one is connected as she is to the life she has made

Everything becomes possible, difficulties seem away to fade

That doesn't mean her way has been easy, Life isn't that nice

But unaffected by whatever troubles encountered, and I've looked,
 I've found no vice

And her friend, of long standing, a constant surprise

With her smile, her calm she must be wise

A traveler, an artist, a mother, with just enough of an edge

She'll speak her mind freely – one doesn't have to dredge

Two dogs, three dogs, four dogs – maybe more

All seem welcome to her home, as if it has no door

So these ladies of the Park who brighten my day

Who provide encouragement to me in the most sincere way

Are precious to me, so we now have a club whose purpose is clear

We are of the 10 who hold this world safe from fear

For if ever our number – though we don't always know who we are

Should drop below 10, the end of this world won't be far

True to ourselves, natural and at ease

Spreading a light the illuminates for real – its no tease

Long may they watch over all those who they love

For their presence is soft and warm like a velvet glove.

WHO IS ME?

May 2017

Normally a question one asks endlessly

During those teenage years, when hopelessly

No answer exists since one has lived but a few years

But obsessively it's asked, nourished by doubts and fears

So unfinished we are at this stage

Theoretically, the answer grows clearer with age

Planning seems an obvious necessity

A spouse, children, a house and prosperity

The years pass as if in some kind of dream

They are mostly good, like eating ice cream

A curve in the road apperrs as the children prepare to leave

Realizing they will never come home for good, I began to grieve

ather, it was to be my defining role

Filling in what I'd missed, making me whole

Strong for my family, no weight was too heavy

Solved every problem for the others, an willing levy

But to awake in one's forties this role on the decline

Who was I to be, which path ahead was to be mine?

With no children around to fill the home

Suddenly thrown back on one's spouse – still together, yet alone

Grown apart, life's early promise fulfilled

The crop had been harvested, the field now untilled

What seed could be planted that could flourish again?

To feel one's individuality resurface, and then

The other, the one we thought we knew

Reveals themselves as different, yet providing no clue

For a mask they had worn, thinking it easier to please

Than to see who they were. How it had become a disease

Of the mind and the heart, growth arrested

Angry demons lashed out, frustrated, detested

\Betrayal in ways deeper than trust

One sought friendship, the other empty lust

For her strength derived from her power to seduce

Or so she thought, the years advancing tightened the noose

To have slept for two decades, making believe

The end was inevitable – one had to leave

It was hard, after so many years two as one

We pushed through it with success, but rarely with fun

I left with my sense of self, of who I'd become

Thanks to the distance I could walk – no need to run

Sure as sure as at this age one can be

I saw my choices in front of me

Built over the years, it was my way

Being open to life, without letting it hold total sway

Learned so much, not all of it nice

There were days of cold pain, and burning ice

A new adventure emerged, though in thinking back

I had prepared it slowly, before the crack

his confidence I'd found, the man I now was

Conscious of what I didn't know, yet sure of what this man does

Children are gone, they are on their own

Father watched over them, how they had grown

His little girls, how he'd wanted them always to be

After all, it was his most fulfilling identity

Life doesn't stand still, one can't plant a tent

It is loaned to us for a time, we only pay rent

No longer needing to compose with anyone

Who was I – no longer father, husband or son?

Into this challenge I devoted myself as I believed good things were meant for me

Renewing my acquaintance with this place I was from, this city

For I had changed in ways unrecognized

Perhaps more Swiss now than American, more civilized?

I'd taken from each the best of both places

So different, neither better, two different races

I'd always been one to live in two worlds at the same time

Comfortable in both, yet neither was mine

Observer and participant, did I pull it off?

I think mostly I did, though some may scoff

As each good thing hides a darker side

What did this seeming self-sufficiency hide?

I think, looking back, I'd always felt alone

Yet to be loved as a child, this too I had known

Though tempered it was with a subtle demeaning tone

There was but one sin for which I might atone

Too caring, too ready others to understand

It was as if my heart was born full, no need more to demand

Was it modesty, or feeling it was the price to be accepted?

Though rarely by others was I ever rejected

No more than anyone else in my state

Though there was an older sister who thrived on hate

This made me different, my values not always a match

Rarely petty, more giving, was I not a catch?

As I entered my life as a newly minted singleton

What did I want really – serious or fun?

An odd mix am I, light-hearted and grave

More often the white knight than some selfish knave

I sing not my praises for my faults are real

But fundamentally I am guided by my heart and how I feel

I live in a time where this is not the way

Other forces drive our lives, sincerity, it seems, has gone astray

And with it, connection, so sought after, yet so rarely found

For without it only selfishness can claim the ground

How then to deal with this environment so ill suited to my kind

For I've invested heavily not only in my heart, but also my mind

This synthesis has brought clarity for I sense and I see

What I've noticed is that when I speak, some flee

I've actually been told "too serious," "too much intensity"

For as a people we've abandoned what's important in favor of petty mondanity

How odd to me it seems when one's path starts to make sense

Our choices multiply, our potential becomes immense

But I am among the few who see things this way

So I live in this world of which I can make sense every day

Appreciated, even admired, yet spreading unease

Even when spoken in humor, those infected with the disease

Of normalcy, holding one's demons in check

As long as the mask holds firmly above the neck.

Have I missed the mark so completely these many years

Though when tragedy struck there was no shortage of tears

And diversity might kick me in the gut

I take it to heart and manage to quickly resurface, but

This faculty that allows me to survive seemingly well

If I try and explain it to others, it remains a hard sell

For it engages forces deep inside

Most prefer from these forces to hide

It is said that at this time of life

When one is alone with no partner or wife

Not to fall to temptations one find's outside

Best to look first and foremost to oneself, inside

My demons, those I perceive

Frighten me no longer for I've come to believe

That they can only hurt me, grow stronger in time

If I disavow them as if they were not mine

The truths they reveal may not open each door

The bricks laid in one's life can't change, even to restore

Nor can one move the foundations, the past remains as before

Though with time we see how at times less is more

But one can come to see the sense of it all

Some newness is possible, life does roll like a ball

So in this time of my life when new challenges I face

When life is lived at a difference pace

The clock is ticking, each day is one less

The race is on, I am forced to confess

Wiser perhaps, knowing I can't have it all

There are times when I'm lost, and the motor seems to stall

No innocent faith in some future that awaits

One who has lived eyes open can't see any pearly gates

But neither do I feel my fate is sealed

It will be, as I live, over time revealed.

WHY WE DO WHAT WE DO

May 2017

Of late I've been struck more and more

In our world where there is so much waiting in store

Choice abounds, perhaps too much in fact

So why does it seem instead of thinking we prefer to simply act?

Appetites define us in ways we don't comprehend

We feed without nourishment, blind to the consequences waiting around the bend

Some say I'm wrong, we think too much

And there maybe some truth to this construct

For thinking alone has a penchant to begin

With a conclusion, then proceeds to commit the same old sin

Of closing the circle, avoiding what does not fit

Tautologies abound, a comfortable chair in which to sit

Obvious truths restated in terms savant, designed to confuse

So we can continue ourselves to abuse

Science advances, charging forward at a frenetic pace

But whoever decided it should be a race?

And what of those who simply act?

They live in a concrete world, that's a fact

But who holds the tiller and in which hand?

No need to justify nor take a consistent stand

No direction emerges, unless it's of egocentricity we speak

The boat advances while no one notices we've sprung a leak

Taking on water, much like growing fat

We all know where that ends, now about other things let's chat

And what of those who look to God for solutions?

Strictly respect the rituals, holidays and ablutions

How can something defined for reasons to which we have lost their meaning?

If such is the case, is now not good time for weaning?

What's left, ah yes, love needs to be considered

How do we look on our emotions – have they thrived or withered?

Their purpose, to imbue with meaning that which we hold
dear

For their inner value, so we hold them near

Unquestioned, these anointed can rule our lives

How many billions in their service have been put to our
knives?

And nowadays, for reasons one can clearly see

Have we lost or found the 'thou," and forgotten to be?

Terms that express an intimacy, small yet great

Reserved for those who together, have joined their fate

It seems to me – though in limited numbers

There are fewer who succeed, and many more stumblers

Love exists in the service of that which we chose

Do we know how to choose wisely, or delegate the selection to
our nose?

To a new invention, beyond simple lust

Chemistry the ineffable, the all knowing, the just

A convenient concept, invented to circumvent

Any serious thinking as to why to one we were meant

When actually, it's quite easy to know

We are attracted to those who complete our show

For everyone see themselves as lacking something

Impossible to have, so we search for a means to bring

The partner we choose most likely has escaped this tarre

So by being together, I can cover my flaws from afar

But if such were the case, why then do so many fail?

Cheat on each other, living their unions as if in jail

Breeding lies, deception, lives destroyed

No, not by this one can we hardly feel buoyed

Yet if a question arises, an answer it deserves

No matter how imperfect – no straight line, only curves

Standing now before the answer's door

The one holding the key to what lies in store

But have you noticed, we look everywhere but here?

I know why – and the answer is almost always fear

Of what, you might ask, and right you would be

Why do I look with eyes shut so I cannot see?

Having taken a brief journey to examine the question

Do any of you have any thoughts or just indigestion?

Why bother with such a tortured reflection? Where might it lead?

And if I just dismiss it from the start, dismiss the subject I won't have
to heed.?

We live in two worlds – one ordered to suit our needs

The other, true reality, on chaos it feeds

The first we created eons ago

To shelter us from the harsh, random, winds that blow.

The second we ignore, so as not to know

To see, incapable of comprehending its flow

For to know is to understand the enormity of it all

Like standing on a tall mountain, dizzy from the height, afraid to fall

We've gotten this far walking past this door

Can we go much further, can we know what for?

To save what we have, to finally understand

What was given can be taken back – this was never our land

It was loaned to us for some purpose we choose to ignore

Will we once have the courage to know what it's forr?

I can't believe this time will not come

If we have eyes, were we not meant to look up at the sun?

Some might respond no, our eyes would burn

Best away from such a light to turn

Yet, if in so doing, do I not choose anything more to learn?

Would that not make pointless here our so short sojourn?

UNWORTHY

November 17, 2012

*T*wo years have gone and come

An unwilling father, a faithless son

Misbegotten products of what love had begun

In joy and caring and innocence and fun

I continue to believe, in spite of my wiser self

That within that seed was a key to happiness and wealth

So much time I've spent trying to understand

Why good goes bad when all that was needed was near at hand

Explanations abound, all true and deep

But the one, the only, the key to it all I could not keep

Return I do from time to time

To ponder the question, an answer to assign

Narcissus rasied his head, that's clear

But that was not a stretch, he was always visibly near

Abandonment, another nail in the box

Marked your heart like some ancient pox

And he who claimed you as his own

His evil seed long ago sown

And then it hit me, the key to it all

Why you turned your eye away from the ball

Love is the answer, but not that which I gave

It was the one you forbade yourself which there to save

All this show of style and allure

A makeup job, no real cure

Self-loathing, the primal blame we dare not name

That's what keeps us out of the game

For if we do not believe that we deserve to find love

Then life is lived like some wounded dove

A broken wing, unable to fly

Il we can do is look up at the forbidden sky

Unworthy, you say, punish your heart

Blame that which is your very best part

Should those around you not see your worth

Then how to discover what is yours from the very day of your birth?

You've searched for some measure, some way to believe you deserve

That which should have been yours; not held in perpetual reserve

To build a life with bricks of sand

Life's tests they cannot withstand

Instead of allowing experience to prove your worthiness

You always end up feeling never truly more, but less

And when you found love where least expected

All you knew to do was to run from it, leave it rejected

The sad story was once again safe, the plot continued unbroken

Your wounded heart remained unbespoken

But I will not abandon what I felt

In spite of it all, I understand the cards you were dealt

I know of your struggles, your heartache and more

I know wherein lie the keys to the door

The answer to why wrong choices your continue to make

Is simple like a recipe for a chocolate cake

Take from what I gave you

It's an ingredient designed to renew

Add a measure of thought

Rekindle the emotion with the yeast you have bought

Mix it with care, love and devotion

Set it aside, letting it rise like the tide in the ocean

It will lift you up from the depths to see

What I saw in you, and all you can be

Say yes at last to your yearning heart

Say yes at last to your better part

Say no to the fear, the doubt and mistrust

Embrace your healthy, hearty lust

It's a taste for life and all which could be yours

If only you walk through the lockless doors

Two years now have past and still I care

I see no sense in it, no reason to dare

Other than without this thing that we shared

Something precious from my life would be pared.

I have tried to find it in other's blank faces

Have even tried to sample other races

But always I return to the same place

The acquamarine eyes, the adorable face

The taste, the smell, the vision of you

The pain, anguish and frustration, they are there too

But like Don Quixote and his foolish dreams

What would become of the world if we all played on the same teams?

Faith, like so many things, is a matter of choice

No proof exists to give it an ultimate voice

But without it life is small and bland

We'd live on a small island, not a continent of endless land

A place where we can believe

And not just exist, survive and then grieve

Joy is what I seek, it is what I found

To find it again, I will search around

I will persevere, assail the high walls

No fear can ever make me small

In sports or life, there is one cardinal sin

Rise up now; believe you can win

Strong from the heart as it was meant to be

I'm here, waiting to see

A new day, a time when you will be free

And perhaps once again, a new us will welcome me.

Not waiting for something which may never arrive

Life rewards those who show they're alive

Who try and put themselves in her way

Like good old Scarlett said – 'Tomorrow is another day"

"We cannot change anything until we accept it. Condemnation does not liberate, it oppresses."

C.G. Jung

Think of this next time you correct a child, reprimand a friend or berate a spouse. If it's really a change you want, is not a thoughtful explanation more effective. But if you give in to your anger, it's no longer about the perpetrator. It's about venting your own anger from the past.

WHERE SHOULD WE BEGIN?

July 2017

Have you ever wondered, when a question is put forth

Where should one begin – east, west, south or north?

Some cardinal points - metaphors, of course

An example: when looking at why a marriage ended in divorce

Were the seeds not there, though blinded by some unknown force

We call it love, celebrated as the only valid reason. It's just the right horse

So why through the years do conflicts appear?

Bringing with them their retinue of insecurity and tears

Did any consider others who might be driving the car?

Were they not perhaps the better indicators of just how far?

Look to the parents, many counsel if so inclined

Were they able to keep their promises, being of similar mind?

Was the father overbearing, emotionally present in some limited way?

And did mother defer to him, or her own game did she play?

For the genders have their roots in biology, perhaps why such exists

One bigger, one stronger, one with breasts and child bearing hips

For in the darkness from which we came

Fertility was the key to survival, the name of the game

Numbers were required for no one could survive on their own

No need for complex anthropological studies, this truth to be known

And so through the ages, as the groups grew in number and strengthCivilization emerged in breadth and length

And to some degree, in behavior these primal forces evolved

In houses not caves were simple gender issues resolved?

Brute force and violence gave way to tastes more refined

Or so it seemed on the surface, but what still lurked in our mind?

When the lights are off and the door is closed

When what happens therein no one beyond these walls knows

What urges return, sometimes complicit, sometimes imposed

Power returns to the context, civilization is deposed

Now back to today when gender issues are discussed with such expertise

Society analyzed most often in terms of disease

Using words pretentious,, scientific, psychological

What gets lost? Oddly, in this case the biological.

Now our physical selves alone the whole story can't tell

For capable we are of doing good things, as well

Grants for studies and books of such goodness simply won't sell

We want to bathe in negation and stories from hell

There is such a thing as a mind, though it's used in limited ways

Serious reflection no longer current, with other things we fill our days

When young people engage and make promises the import they ignore

They have no idea of what truly lies in store

Experience too short, self-awareness too thin

A promise for life can quickly turn into a sin

So what is the answer? What is the point?

Have I lost you all by now – fleeing the joint?

When considering any matter of import great or small

The place to begin, to start rolling that ball

Is not in the middle, like walking with one leg

Life lived thusly can become a dangerous powder keg

Who knows what's inside, how volatile it might be

Love does blind – it's clear for all to see

Each marriage in fact or in name

Like some game board, having many pieces, yet by no means tame

Things from the parents, things of their own

Societies myths, and the experience of life that they've known

Multiplied by two, each piece of the equation

That makes for a very diverse and volatile nation

Where the meeting's mediator – sex - cannot bear the burden it's given

Over time fails as it must, in so many directions the marriage is driven

Intimacy, trust, fidelity – challenges for which one is rarely prepared

And perhaps most important of all, knowing why at the start one cared

If asked, what might young lovers say?

Why did you chose this one on that fateful day?

The answer a woman might give could go like this

He's smart, he's handsome, he's got money and he's funny – bliss!

And the man, his answer would begin with her looks

She's hot, good in bed, love sex – perfect, like in the books

To dress it all up and not be left on the hook

"We love each other" – and that's all that it took

So there you have it, the foundation on which to build a marriage

Seems a bit creaky to me, like some horse drawn carriage

End of the example, I've no idea from whence it came

When writing poetry I'm rarely in charge – it's just the game

But the point is clear for all to see

If you want a chance to realize life's promise and be

That person you used to dream about – a glorious "me"

Those treasures of all kinds await - but they are not for free

At least ask yourself "why" more often, know the reasons hidden
from easy view

Don't fear the secrets as if their origins and purpose you really knew

Start at the place where it all began

The same holds true for a woman or man

To start in the middle of any reflection

Promises but one thing, failure and the absence of any clear
direction

It's building on sand, moving and unstable

You'll have no idea what's shaking the table

The dishes will slide, some crashing to the floor

And you might even start rushing for the door

Don't be fooled by the experts whose knowledge is narrow and thin

Reflecting today's truths, yet ignoring their origin

There is a wealth of wisdom in the experience of our kind

Erroneous conclusions, stilted language, and a laughable find

But it took all of that to land in today's place

Thanks to our mind and some divine grace

Indeed we've come far – obvious from the trail of our mistakes

It's the wisdom we've paid for, that's what it takes.

No shortcuts, no expedience, no superficiality

That's the deceptive path of fantasy, not reality.

Follow it if you will, for a time, play a part if that 3hat you want to be

But no role ever set anyone free

Endorsed by experts, the data says so

Just follow the directions, you don't have to know

What lives in the black box, the algorithm at work

What's really included in the analyses and the biases that lurk?

Have you heard the expression "…garbage in, garbage out?"

If nothing else, at the very least, nourish a healthy doubt

Does this mean there is no one to trust

All those declarations, are they all meant to just stir up the dust?

To confuse, to imply, to reassure and mislead

All "sold" for one purpose, so their advice you will heed

You may say you've neither time nor, the expertise

To do your own research to find the origin of your own disease

To learn used to be something we aspired to do

But today it seems there's no taste for it, just act as if you knew

For an opinion suffices, or so I've been told

One young man once said he needed no fact a position to hold

His view was worth the same and that of anyone

No argument, no fact, could dissuade this son

Why know when you can believe? – it's more fun

And if knowledge is discounted, what argument can't be won?

So off he went, ignorance embraced

And if representative of his generation, we are all debased.

No census of the mind have I taken

But my confidence in the future was shaken

Let's hope I'm wrong, facts we won't ignore

Though it does sound a bit like 1984

FOR HEAVEN'S SAKE

From the Chris/Hank Series

June 2017

You think to control your heart by freezing it cold

When all it does is make you prematurely old

Cynics - those who embrace hope that is lost

Too afraid to believe in their dreams, by life too violently tossed

But something survives buried within you deep

The hill to climb looks now perhaps too steep

But here I am, my hand always there

You know that with my help, you can dare

Revive those dreams, feel the rush they provide

Step into the sunshine, you've no longer need to hide

Your shackles of dark illusions, aside them cast

They don't have to live in your future; they belong in your past

A new voice, a new message, one in tune with your heart's current place

Though much time seems wasted, this is not some race

But a quest, your salvation, the future you secretly seek

The one that still frightens you each time you see but a peek

Too close to the truth – your truth – did you come?

Joy, excitement, love, fun

The world on its head, you chose dark over light

You put down your arms before taking up the fight

Faith needs hope to survive

Each time with the latter, you bury the former alive

These are matters where reason has little sway

Emotions see more clearly, they point the way

When doubt leads to fear, fear abandons love

Yet when it's needed, as they did for Noah, come the doves

Soft and gentle, neither harsh nor filled with hate

Bringing back into focus the very next gate

Will courage emerge giving birth to faith?

Will the angel appear or the ancient wraith?

What is that thing that will get you over the line?

And will it arrive just in time?

Imperfect, unsure, the future's an uncharted land

Yet be certain of the unfailing, caring, offered hand

Will it be taken, is the time now right?

Or does darkness still obscure the remnants of your light?

All I know is what I've said

Like seeds, my words are planted once they are read

This is the way I know how to do

This is the way, tried and true

This is the way, my part I fulfill

This is the way, embrace your dream, feel the thrill

Find some way to make it last.

Abandon the darkness, end the fast

To find a reason to live, stop spiting yourself

To think that those who betrayed you care for your health

If they left you once so long ago

Why let this evil seed continue to grow?

They cared not then, they care less now

Why to this evil totem do you continue to bow?

Revenge won't bring back what was never there

These people don't know what it means to care

You chase your tail like some animal crazed

Wounded, bleeding, clothed in failure – yet still amazed

That this is the road taken, the one that got you here

Has it brought you what you want? Are you more near?

The answer you know, it's letting go you ignore

I showed you the way, even led you to the door

This feeling, this legacy, this irresistible force

Unloved once unloved always – it controls your course

So disappear once again, I have once again failed

You love your cross and remain to it nailed

Is the failure mine or is it yours

I can't make you go through the doors

the vortex has once again drawn you in

You have not the strength to choose, there's your sin

Caught in an every repeating loop

Lower and lower you go in a stoop

A posture you should no long accept

But then if you steal to survive, it remains a theft

You sleep in the subway, your direction without goal

How in these conditions can you save your soul?

To bounce back and forth between hope and despair

This is no way to live, it's simply not fair

Like all circles, this one has no beginning or end

There is but one solution, your life to mend

Cut the string you believe is meant to last

The threads of your life, you mind, are unraveling fast

None can live the life you've lived for long

I can't imagine the pain, the longing to belong

To have a home, a safe place to sleep

And a job, some money, some things you can keep

Not live with your few things hidden here and there

To be stolen by others like you, when they dare

The chances of seeing you one day free

When we can speak of your future, it could be

Though small, the light now too weak to be seen

I am here to prove to you all life is not meant to be mean

So wherever you are, I hope you take care

Try and worry less about losing your hair

And in those moments when your anger takes a break

Hold fast to my words, please, for heaven's sake.

SOMEBODY, ANYBODY, NOBODY

July 2017

I've become a student of sex in our time

It's a subject that seems to preoccupy everyone's mind

It's the foundation – supposedly – of every good relation

And blessed by all churches, God, and the entire nation

So much has been written making so little sense

Advice, however expert, seems amateur to me and makes everyone tense

So let's start from scratch and take a big step back

To follow my own advice, that's the best way to stay on track

There are many ways to begin this exploration

Psychology, medicine, technique – all part of the equation

I prefer to start with the players, the who not the how

It's a different approach, but forgotten it seems for now

If you see yourself in a balanced way

If you are not too insecure, frustrated or had a rough day

Whatever the reason – most prefer to ignore

You're edgy, even horny, and staring at the door

Your desire has no object that's set in stone

Like so many – married or otherwise – too often feeling alone

You have to get out, find someone with whom to connect

The question becomes then where to go and how to select

If confidence reigns, and colleagues have told you you're hot

Go look for a 10, don't sit on the pot

For you are somebody, your attributes are clear

They must be obvious to everyone, so have no fear

If success doesn't greet you quickly enough

If the prospects for the evening start to look rough

Maybe you're aiming too high – a nine?

What the hell – we'd go down – a four or a five might be fine

Still no luck, this is getting serious, what to do?

There are more fives than tens, who are very few

So resolved to find someone acceptable, more or less

What the hell, it's just sex. Go for it. God bless

So now we're looking for almost anybody

I won't tell my friends they weren't a hottie

What would define their ranking, their class?

Who cares if they're flat chested or have no ass?

Secure in the knowledge that I'm slumming a bit

Sex with anybody, it's just a one time fit

But what if that's all I meet, one anybody after another

Those qualities that made me a ten – each time do I smother?

Forgetting those things that I value, that truly make me me

The first victim of sex with anybodies is my sincerity

Most often we close our eyes, feigning some passionate reaction

Our mind's eye on the clock, hoping for a quick satisfaction

If it comes first for me, after all that's what I was after

Who cares if were exchanged no words or laughter?

We dress, lie that we'll speak again soon

And head out into the night to find that old friend – the lonely moon

What comes of a succession of anybodies after a time?

Is there beginning to appear a hole in that soul of mine?

An emptiness.s spreading darkness, even despair

What's wrong, everyone tell me I have great hair?

For what has happened, what this journey has wrought

Is a dark prize no one ever wanted, but was bought

To forget you are somebody is to walk a dark road

It's like throwing away the best of you - like some beautiful lawn
badly mowed

Once that has happened, an anybody you've become

No more tens in your future, not even one

For you've downgraded yourself, there's no one else to blame

So carry on this road, always the same

Since sex is meaningless, after all

It's just another booty call

Like a good bowel movement, once a day

I guess that's all there is on the subject to say

But is the endpoint, one can't descend any more?

Too many anybodies and there remains yet another, lower, floor

It's the world of nobodies, those who've lost their soul

No more of those qualities remain that made you whole

Is there a way back, one can almost always find a way

Ah , but yes, there is a price to pay

To reclaim what was lost requires admitting what you've done

And realize that the meaning of life is not 'hot, now and fun.'

For that's what happened, people have themselves reduced

To an accessory, sold on sale, with the packaging juiced

To feed a fantasy, since reality is no more

Emptied of any value, sex quickly becomes a bore

Forgotten is the girt if valued it can be

Quality over quantity – ah the paucity

For it has become about body parts and roles

As long as there are the requisite number of holes

To select and use, a veritable Chinese menu of delight

For the conversation that should be sex is now a plight

How to be sure you get the items selected?

No question of anything being questioned or rejected

"What do you mean?" It's what I like

"What's wrong with you – you must be a dyke."

I could go on, please excuse the expressions

They are there for color and to indicate the general direction

Two people meet and want to share in pleasure

Is serial use of each other the path to the treasure

Where is the discovery, the trust, the vulnerable soul?

That one allows another to touch, making them feel whole

Deepening the connection instead of casting a wide net

Hoping to find another lost soul who also lost their bet

That one day Prince Charming or Sleeping Beauty

Will arrive on the scene, with her sublime booty

You'll fall into each others arms forever

Wake up sweetheart, it's more like never

Anything of value takes time to weave

There must be the conviction not to leave

Imperfection is inherent in us all

It can make life more interesting, and not necessarily small

So if sex is what you think is the key

Go for it and shortly you will see

Things go flat much too quickly

And sex becomes more and more prickly

For if an orgasm is really all you have to say

That really isn't much in the way

Of a conversation that can grow in scope

Leaving in its wake very little hope

\So courage my friends, forget all you've heard

Set it free and hope it will fly away like some bird

Think of what sex is really all about

Speak from your heart and begone foul doubt

WARMTH AND PEACE

May 2017

When in my search, no one do I find

A shift occurs in my mind

The stars which emanate from my heart

Their constellation's clarity seems to fall apart

The pieces which began as a coherent whole

Split into disparate pieces, each with its separate role

One goes primal, all lust and thirst

To take what it wants, it alone exists, its needs come first

The object, no longer a person, is there for one reason

To suit my mood, my hunger, my season

No significance in my acts, however violent or tame

It's forgotten as soon as it's over, the whole thing lame

For my choice is driven by bits and pieces

It's all about now, divergent needs and their singular releases

Pleasure is to be mine alone, and for a time that's brief

It's a bodily function, nothing more – just plain simple relief

And like some physiological need

When it comes, one must heed

But is that what this is about?

I am – and want to be – more just than some lout

If sex exists for more than one reason

If two join as one for more than a season

It's not societies conceit

No culture can impose such a feat

We value ourselves for our language – written and spoken

It places us – in our minds – above all others – sounds to me broken

Language is expression, and as such is shared by all creation

Time to let some air out of our inflated selves – how about some deflation?

Anyone who knows animals of any sort

Anyone who's watch them live and cavort

No words are spoken – at least that we understand

But so much more is said and it's really quite grand

We call it body language for to us foreign it's become

Value our words so highly, we have forgotten where we're from

There was a time when communication had no words

We screeched and grunted like pigs and birds

Watching expressions to divine intent

Words came much later to enhance, not invent

How far we have strayed from our roots in so many ways

We fill our heads too often with nonsense – as we do our days

Who truly observes nowadays how the body speaks?

One could say dancers and artists and other artistic "freaks"

The body is the house inhabited by our minds

It takes us where we need to go allowing adventures of all kinds

To live just as mind, with no body – how weird

Let's stick with this union, the alternative is to be feared

So back to sex, it's the language our body speaks

The problem resides in the fact that we've become the freaks

It's all in our words which fail us when intimacy calls

Add emotion to the mix, all meaning falls

Overwhelmed by sensation and closeness, our roots take hold

The forms that sex can take can make one's blood run cold

It's really quite simple, look at it like this

Why does real sex begin with a kiss?

Something tender, articulate with no word spoken

An exchange, desires are silently spoken

If one listens with one's heart, it all becomes clear

Until someone awakens, are we getting too near?

A primal fear when the borders start to melt

Yet isn't that what happens when we've joined and felt

Two become one, when time itself does cease

Nothing else exists but the warmth of each other, and peace

Are there words that can express what the body can say?

It's violent expressions are only regressions, when frustration exacts
its pay

Take something normal, in the center it lives

Deprive it of freedom and spontaneity and watch what gives

Slowly but surely, desire turns dark

The purr starts to change into a bark

Desire becomes a hunger that won't be denied

Love is replaced by aggression and pride

It's a dark path too many follow, having lost their way

And for that a darkness descends on their day

So ponder these thoughts if so inclined

Refer to your too often excluded heart, not just your mind

Set aside your fear your true self might be seen

Release your senses, let them grow keen

A new world will awaken not all about release

And that warmth I spoke of earlier, let it bring you peace.

WORDS, AGAIN

July 2017

I've written about words before

Thinking that it would once and for all close that door

On a subject so present in all that we do

I'd just assumed everyone knew'

Of all of the creatures that walk, fly or swim

And though many communicate above the din

There is but one who has formed a lexicon

The essential element our species relies upon

Our language is what combines our minds

Even if those languages are of different kinds

Syntaxe for structure, semantic for meaning

Together they have enabled us from nature our weaning

To rise above the here and the now

To preserve for the future the acquired know how

In short, words are the mind's tools

And like them, one can use them wisely or like fools

In the past, I believe, words were designed to impress

Great orations were given, often under great duress

To inspire listeners to rise to the occasion

And to speak articulately allowed many to rise above their born
station

For intelligence needs tools to grow and build

Without them, fields lie fallow, the mind's soil untilled

But something has happened, since when is hard to know

Like a virus in some program, a dulling wind does blow

Causing us to relax, abandoning precision

Colloquial, idiosyncratic, entertaining, division

The lines which serve to define the meaning of things

No one seems to miss the precision it brings

We sort of get it, going back to the day

When we had too few words to be able to say

And be sure that our words were both heard and understood

Without it things could never be as they should

An example of interest that happened today

A political discussion on the politics of the day

Of a President who uses words to confuse

Successful he is since who knows if it's ignorance or ruse

Healthcare was the subject, debated between the parties concerned

Both of whom agreed in principal but on an inappropriate word, the conversation turned

One, having lived in Europe for many a year

Familiar with their ways, formed by experience and fear

Solidarity has guided how society treats its populace

Taxed higher perhaps, few freedoms lost, causing little distress

Free healthcare, free education, pensions and more

"That's Socialilsm" cried one participant, as if he'd just learned his wife was a whore

So I asked him, dear friend, what exactly do you mean?

Socialism is a word full of emotion, abhorred by our team

Oddly enough, unable to define the word he did choose

Progress, though careful not to let him think the argument he did lose

"We don't want Socialism" stated as if the Devil himself had spoken

But did he consider that their system works and ours is broken?

Observation is another of those words, tricky to use

The susceptible hear judgment – something difficult to defuse

For one can observe making no claims, seeking only to point something out

To nourish a conversation or clear up some doubt

I could go on, the examples don't lack

The point is when a word is misused, it often leads to an attack

So what has happened, how did rigor get so sick

To see the certainty it used to bring, cut short the wick

Perhaps that's it, when precision fails

Like dogs that are frightened, they pull in their tails

Ignorance is indeed a fearful state

Quickly giving way to anger and hate

The circle grows vicious as words don't bring us to a clearer place

And the downward spiral accelerates its pace

To our most basic instincts of survival and defense

The past and the future are forgotten, only remains the present tense

From words of wisdom from statesmen wise

Thugs have now taken over and other "wise guys"

This has happened before – facism being the most recent case

Where words were deformed in their meaning and nearly wiped out a race.

So all of you people who speak all day long

Pause for a moment and listen to yourselves, and just how very wrong

When you explain a thought, do you sound like a fool

Less concerned with informing than sounding cool

The conversations one hears as others speak on their phone

I often think no one is really listening, so not much to atone

But there will be times when a thought will require precision

When humor and sarcasm in the service of derision

Will cause an eruption of an emotional kind

Because speakers lack the words, serving the ignorant mind

Read to your children, teach the well

Not just grammar and how to spell

Give them the tools to grow their minds

Require they respect each meaning, as treasured finds

And you will see how their world will grow

Beyond the frivolous preoccupations they too well know

They will reach beyond the place where they live

And we will all benefit from the gift our words can give.

WHAT TO MAKE OF GUILT?

July 2017

Guilt itself has many faces

It's influence broad, just follow its traves

An emotion perhaps closer to awareness

For we spoken of it as one of life's harness'

Most think of it in a moral sense

Cultural authorities define it to serve their interests in the present tense

But like emotions of a complex nature

It's understanding, so necessary, comes from the past but directs the future

One face is clear, when we transgress some rule

Defined from the outside, its enforcement can be cruel

Its purpose resides in protecting us all

One can wonder if its opposite is praise some tool

In the service of the goals and objectives a society desires

Sanctions can go from a slap on the hand to burning alive in fires

So this kind of guilt, imposed from the outside

And enforced often doggedly leaving no place to hide

Having little to no control of these dictates collective

As long as we stay clear of them, it's live and let live

Now the other kind of guilt of interest here

Comes from a source more interior and near

Its purpose should not be repressive, that's not what its about

It's a voice from within, ready to shout

If and when we stray from the essentials , more feeling than laws

Nevertheless can leave us for years in the grip of its jaws

IT'S NOT FAIR

July 2017

Most of my life as an adult

When tested, never tempted by a cult

Believing that God was still and always there

And would know that I do care

Truly and deeply and not for my life

Through the years I felt protected from danger and strife

From the ordinary evil that happens every day

We all have our lot to assume, to bear it and never say

"It's Not Fair" when those we love must suffer

And pay some exorbitant price with no buffer

But most of all when an innocent is chosen

My heart hurts as if it was frozen

Do we all get only a fixed number of passes?

When it's 50/50 and we come out winners in our classes

I've counted down each one, not knowing how many were   left

But in the past few years I've lost too much and feel bereft

I've tried making deals with the Divine

Offering that he takes from me what little that is mine

An eye for a life, a year for a pet

And it seems he takes both and shows no regret

I've managed until now

Not to give in and bow

To the thought that he perhaps he did not see

Nor hear each and every plea

When I raise my eyes up to the sky

Asking him for some reason why

Knowing there is none, that life isn't fair

Or is it that He simply doesn't care

Rational thoughts seek a way not to give in

To deny Him – would that not be a sin?

Do I fear to take the step and say no more can I believe?

When from the depths of my sadness all that remains is grieve

Where to find the hope that bridges these times

When all that there seems to be are the fines

To be paid in currencies of all kinds

Yet at some point do they run dry the mines?

I ask myself what is there more to lose?

Chaos is that the worst He could choose?

There is always more He could take

If I say the word and forsake

So each time my heart is broken

Each time he refuses my offer, my token

To save another and take from me

I step up to the line but cannot see

What lies on the other side

And once again, I lengthen my stride

My heart starts to heal

But the loss I will always feel

Childish to consider myself the one responsible for it all?

How could I possibly prevent or stop another's fall?

But somehow I feel I must try

Yet resignation each time passes me by

No saint am I, for this must come from me

Did I feel this so early and oh so deeply?

But after Lily, do You really need Will?

Is heaven so short of sweet souls that You must fill?

Taking the beauty, the love and loyalty

From this world where we are already drowning in cruelty

I can make no sense, yet sense there must be

How is it through this sadness I cannot see?

So once again back from the brink I walk

I'll find some kernel of hope and talk

To He who, if He is still there

And ask Him not to hurt yet another innocent, hoping He still knows how to care.

No negotiation, no exchange, nothing offered was enough

But love for Him, I'm not sure I've still got the right stuff.

So one last time, please spare this poor boy

He has suffered in life and finally found some joy

His innocence of heart and the heart that has never run dry

Leave him here to finish his time, don't take him away to the sky

The FORTRESS

June 2017

In early life when challenged by an event

Wherever they come from, by whomever they were sent

Our response, built over the years

Are defensive walls, to keep us safe – their mortar, our fears

These walls start small, just large enough

It takes time to feel life's assaults and threatening stuff

Each time we're shaken, unsure

We add another level, as if to cure

Fears don't disperse once left behind

Inevitably more come be they of a different or similar kind

Sooner or later, from atop this now high wall

We can look to the distance believing we're now safe from it all

And so it may be, at least for a time

Proud of our edifice, safe behind it, we'll be fine

Life may continue, all things normal may appear

This fortress of mine will protect me from every fear

Through Life we may wander, no one ever sees

Loneliness grows, yet there is no discernible disease

Why is it nothing seems to make me feel

In such a state, am I even real?

My public face reveals no fault or flaw

Why then is there this emptiness, from the inside does it gnaw?

And then it dawns on, I realize

I'd never noticed how high the walls had grown, my fortriess, it's true
 size

Though safe I may be, safe within

Unknowingly, I'd built it with sin

What my impregnable fortress that mocked all trouble

Had become nothing less than my prison – an isolationist bubble

We were not put here to want only to be secure

Isolation alone can provide that, yet for it there is no cure

Remove vulnerability, no connection can be found

I may be safe, but my ship will have run aground

To be touched requires an openness I'd lost

Only over time was revealed its true cost

I remember the time, many years ago

When this truth I'd discovered, I'd come to know

I was told something was wrong, I'd ceased to grow

Like a rock standing rigid when the wild winds blow

As if dead inside, I had no inkling this could be true

Until I saw it clearly, and then I knew

To find my vulnerability again, to break down the wall

I spoke of it to others to know if they'd also heard its call

Amazed I was, their reactions were often the same

No one wanted to hear of it – that component we'd prefer to tame

Better to be safe, for hearts can break

And what of all those "others," those who seek only to take?

I could suffer, should I fear this more than alone?

Or do hearts not grow wiser whilst their sins they atone?

I told my children when of age they came

Fear not to love, broken hearts heal well, it's part of the game

Know this, on this Earth we call home

There is no such thing as a safe place, no neutral zone

Life has one rule that we must never break

Live fully, and to do that, you must participate.

ASHES

July 2017

I was up in my garden in Sullivan County

Admiring my garden and all its bounty

Though I don't spend that much time anymore up there

It's become a bit of a sanctuary of those for whom I care

Since my return to New York and acquired some land

My intention was to set down routes and work with my hands

And so I did, though many people have come and left

All except my faithful and loving pets

Though dogs may grow old, grow up they can't do

Never to leave us, always faithful, we are always but two

This state of dependence contains a unique reciprocity

Where else can one find such unique loyalty?

First there was Nina, many called her Miss

For she was reserved, aloof, but ready with her kiss

She offered me continuity upon my return

And a love for garbage in the city did she learn

And then there was Ares, rescued from the street

He looked ferocious, but was terribly sweet

He loved to carry things in his mouth – be they leash or stick

Though he'd often drop them on the way, and we'd return them up to pick

Nina got sick and a miracle occurred

She dodged a bullet, and I thought our future was secured

Barely two years passed, another cancer declared

And tried what we could, though not better she fared

One summer day in the garden, lying by the pond in the shade

A favorite spot of hers, when I noticed she'd started to fade

We rushed home to the emergency room

But on the way, she met her doom

Expired just like that, in silence and peace

She never complained, but was ready for her final release

I couldn't let her go, it's become a tradition

Some special tree or plant in a favored place – to recall her condition

I asked God to watch over her as it was something I could no longer do

And to send me a sign that she was fine, so that I knew

In the first weeks following her demise

As I sought some solace to make me wise

I noticed a deer – a doe – running in the field next door

She came often and looked my way, and my heart felt less poor

For Nina had returned to life in another form

And I had my sign, Nina was alright, as if reborn

Ares the brave, the stout the loving

When food was produced, there was a fair amount of shoving

But with a heart as big as his outsized head

I knew I was to lose him, a thought I came to dread

For in his simplicity, he was a pillar to me

In my darkest hours, I knew faithful he would always be

Rescued and grateful for the home he had found

When tossed to and fro, now love did surround

But in his 12th year, a lameness took hold

I consulted many a specialist, but no one knew nor told

What was wrong, why he suffered and could not pee

For three days I fretted until finally

Though he didn't move, his urines did flow

I celebrated his rebirth, little did I know

Given his age, and what Nina had endured

No way was I going to adopt extreme measure to have him cured

The next day was dark, my children all came to say goodbye

The vet, a sensitive soul, proceeded to try

One injection to calm him, a second to end it all

His brave heart refused to stop, or even to stall

A second injection put an end to his life

At least he'd had his time and lived without strife

I've since learned that his breed has a vulnerability

Why did no one think to speak of it at the time to me?

At his passing, to honor the time we had shared I wanted a tree

Something tall and strong and also lovely

A Hinkoki Cypress was to be his kind

For he was a blessing in body and mind.

And then there was Lily, love incarnate

There was a faculty I'd never seen before, and it was innate

A sense of giving that knew no bounds

And I've had several Afghan hounds

I've loved them all – each was unique

They moved gracefully and with their eyes did they speak

I've spoken of Lily in other poems, I still feel the pain

My heart was broken; the experience brought me no gain

I saw death come and steal a beautiful soul

Leaving nothing – that's the point – but one very dark hole

Time has softened this journey of death

Though I will never forget when He took her last breath

The point of this is not to blame

What would be the point? One cannot loss, reframe

It must be born with the same dignity shown by the departed

And not let it define for all time the brokenhearted.

I did find a way to make some sense of this fact of life

That wisdom requires pain, loss and strife

For this world is hard and life unfair

If accepted as such, and one does dare

To give when one can, to those in need

There are those who can benefit, different from those driven by greed

The former can learn and grow

The latter seek only to feed

Learn to know the difference between the two

The latter are many, the former are few

The former absorb the warmth that comes from within

The latter, sadly, do not learn, knowing only how to sin

And in the end, when my time has come

I've imagined how to rejoin the Sun

Take my ashes, with those of my dogs, and blend them all as one

On a windy day find a special place, where Life was begun

Washed clean of all impurity

No sense of pain or pity

No darkness lies before us visible to me

Then set us free, so together we can walk for all eternity

SEPARATION

July 2017

Can parents see their children as today they are?

Nor do we recognize how they've changed, live they near or far

It's only in living daily that clarity comes at last

But sometimes old dreams may rule – dark shadows they can cast

Clouding things more, as we labor every day

Trying to do our best, and keep the danger away

The hardest thing to recognize, all parents that we be

The most obvious need a child has, and the hardest for us to see

Is that of separation, when one becomes two

I'm not sure who is more frightened – me, them or you

But Nature requires this division, and so it must be

For every being under creation, in its own way must learn to be free

To live under another – though security and protection are assured

Becomes an impediment to growth – the one thing that must be secured

Time advances and with it, children must learn what it means to be an adult

If this progression is somehow blocked, the child could join a cult

Not one of formal beliefs, with priests and sacraments

Rather a litany of failure, and unending predicaments

Their purpose is clear for all, save a parent that cannot see

For the image they've retained is of the child that used to be

Growth is progressive, no one sees it day by day

And yet there are so many clues that speak but do not say

Odd how we look at them and speak of how they've grown

But knowing who they are today remains the great unknown

The fault lies not only with a parent's loving care

Children growing up are hardly ever fair

Their love is transferred from home to friends outside

With secrets designed truth to replace, deform and hide

Some can transition without too much trouble, for reasons diverse

This is indeed a singular phase for which one cannot reheqrse

Others, less fortunate, perhaps never having learned

To speak their thoughts openly, or by their parents have been burned

Yet, even if the cost is high, and a mighty struggle ensues

Life is not often fair and always demands her dues

Rarely paid in on installment, rather in daily amounts

That it happens for real is what truly counts

No child is saved by sentiment, by love or discipline

The field may be scattered with the wounded, but one side must win

No longer tied to another – be it spouse, sibling or parent

The journey has begun under other roofs or some simple tent

And if the sack they carry contains more than just some things

A spirit thirsty for life inside, forward on this road of kings

The kernel of identity, small though destined to grow

If you have taught them early and well, they will come to know

More each day of who they are, with a purpose to be found

Experience will nourish them and for their future a solid ground

But if the split is missed, and trouble takes its place

Life is long and lived daily – chasing answers at some frenetic pace

Children know when they are lost, and search will they do

But with nothing learned inside to guide them, victories may be few

The child must learn to live alone – it's Nature's first law

To fend for itself, to fight its battles using any means – mind, tooth or claw

Step back, hold fast to your conviction, leave the child alone

Let them pay for their sins, for them they must atone

Mistakes committed on the way the best lessons they provide

If they have learned to own their faults, and not from them to hide

To say it's me, understanding how they were wrong

Not to find another to whom the fault can belong

The lessons we remember best, the ones that longest last

Cost us most and were paid for, slowly not fast

And with their penitence, a new road is revealed

If all goes well and each play their part – the relationship can be healed.

But if for reasons clear, anchored in the past

Their struggles go on too long, on their lives a shadow cast

Life is not fair and the reasons why the road for some is long

Think long and hard why theirs has proven such a difficult song

If you can see through the night, and come to know the reason

I speak not of some easy answer for that would be treason

The truth hurts most before its known

Deprived of understanding, resentful it has grown

For it has lived its life in shadow

Longing only for you to know

How hard it is to watch one's child struggle to find its way

When from the day it was born, we swore protection every day

To ease their path, smooth out their setbacks, challenges them deprive

How easy it is to forget what it means to be alive

Hold fast to the promise unspoken but never made

The one abandonment was forever forbade

There may be times of silence, when separation can work its spell

With Time and Distance mixed together, things may work out well

Perhaps not for the parents, whose life now too must be their own

Their seed was planted, cared for perhaps imperfectly, but it has nonetheless grown

Into something unrecognized, different from one's youthful dreams

But isn't that the point, each life belongs to but one person, or at least to me it seems.

TWO CLOCKS

May 2017

What will you do?

When trust and sincerity are so new?

When they seem to come at you so fast

Will your courage fail? Will it last?

Will it help you see past what came before?

Will you ever be able to find the right door?

Will the words spoken from those you've known?

Will you recognize through their meaning, how much you've grown?

Will you understand why I am here?

Will you be able to look at me without fear?

Will the years that separate our lives?

Will they drive a wedge between us like knives?

Or

Will they help to keep open the door?

To what might, for you, lie in store?

To something as yet unnamed

That will render your demons tamed

And me, who do you see?

And what will define who you will be?

Will your eyes be open and free?

Will in your place grow a bush or a tree?

Or confounded by some unfriendly thought?

Still in the past's web caught?

The way to the future lays in one choice

Will you listen to that inner voice?

The song it sung, the one that led you back

Was it a new or an old track?

Rebounding from another disappointment?

Looking for a bandaid or some soothing ointment?

Our inner voices come from different places

They can be false or true, we must watch their faces

Look closely to where they point

To drown you heart or your head to anoint?

Be sure to ask them at the same time

Whose future is chosen when approaching the finish line

The one that must be crossed

Leaving the familiar past, now hopefully lost

To enter a place undefined

Your undiscovered riches ask but to be mined

Everyone claims no problem exists

With as much thought, they make their bucket lists

Of all that will be theirs

In some future free from cares

Until they face that line

To leave their world and enter mine

Or so it may appear

Until how much the unknown they really fear

For this new world is not only mine

It's a world that awaits each of us in time

One face of the clock marks the past

With a sky mixed, though more often overcast

Don't wait for some certainty from any forecast

Long-term predictions never last

One step at a time, feet solidly planted

Let reality perceived be your guide, not by fantasy enchanted

One guiding image leading the way

Stay loyal to it and you will have your day

But if you fail, if you cling to this past

There is but one thing certain to last

Casting your net in the same waters devoid of hope

Life will always answer you with a resounding "NOPE"

The familiar, reassuring, each day he knows what to wear

Same old clothes, so easy to prepare

Familiar a prison can become

When failed courage blocks the sun

The other face, scarey perhaps, as yet unknown

Isn't that the point; its a field waiting to be sown

What grows depends only on you

A life of freedom, strange and new.

Perhaps more work, much uncertainty

Challenges abound, even difficulty

But this life is yours, and yours alone

The sins of the past can be gone; nothing more to atone

The world awaits your coming, you have much to say

Its up to you a pledge to affirm, "… I want to live and I'm here to stay."

Say yes, and watch things happen, as your vitality grows

Say no, life withers, no passionate wind blows

Say yes, the well will never run dry

Say no, little remains but a fruitless try

So many thoughts and questions, or so it may appear

When taken together, what do you hear?

A single voice, a message clear

The only thing in your way is your own FEAR.

THE FORTRESS

June 2017

In early life when challenged by an event

Wherever they come from, by whomever they were sent

Our response, built over the years

Are defensive walls, to keep us safe – their mortar, our fears

These walls start small, just large enough

It takes time to feel life's assaults and threatening stuff

Each time we're shaken, unsure

We add another level, as if to cure

Fears don't disperse if once left behind

Inevitably more come be they of a different or similar kind

Sooner or later, from atop this now high wall

We can look to the distance believing we're now safe from it all

And so it may be, at least for a time

Proud of our edifice, safe behind it, we'll be fine

Life may continue, all things normal may appear

This fortress of mine will protect me from every fear

Through Life we may wander, no one ever sees

Loneliness grows, yet there is no discernible disease

Why is it nothing seems to make me feel

In such a state, am I even real?

My public face reveals no fault or flaw

Why then is there this emptiness, from the inside does it gnaw?

And then it dawns on, I realize

I'd never noticed how high the walls had grown, my fortriess, it's true size

Though safe I may be, safe within

Unknowingly, I'd built it with sin

What my impregnable fortress that mocked all trouble

Had become nothing less than my prison – an isolationist bubble

We were not put here to want only to be secure

Isolation alone can provide that, yet for it there is no cure

Remove vulnerability, no connection can be found

I may be safe, but my ship will have run aground

To be touched requires an openness I'd lost

Only over time was revealed its true cost

I remember the time, many years ago

When this truth I'd discovered, I'd come to know

I was told something was wrong, I'd ceased to grow

Like a rock standing rigid when the wild winds blow

As if dead inside, I had no inkling this could be true

Until I saw it clearly, and then I knew

To find my vulnerability again, to break down the wall

I spoke of it to others to know if they'd also heard its call

Amazed I was, their reactions were often the same

No one wanted to hear of it – that component we'd prefer to tame

Better to be safe, for hearts can break

And what of all those "others," those who seek only to take?

I could suffer, should I fear this more than alone?

Or do hearts not grow wiser whilst their sins they atone?

I told my children when of age they came

Fear not to love, broken hearts heal well, it's part of the game

Know this, on this Earth we call home

There is no such thing as a safe place, no neutral zone

Life has one rule that we must never break

Live fully, and to do that, you must participate.

THE LIGHT

August 2017

There is indeed a light inside

I've known it's there by my side

Since I was small and saw things clear

And since then, I've kept it near

Its purpose is my path to guide

Though at times it seemed to hide

If lost, not sure of which path was mine

It kept me true with its shine

And if I needed from this course to stray

I knew it was never far away

For even if mistakes I made

I knew for sure afterwards, this path for me was forbade

So here I am, looking from the top of the hill

Most issues dealt with, no outstanding bill

Except the one that has escaped me from the start

To find another with whom to share my heart

I've turned this over a thousand times

It even brought me here, to my rhymes

The light in me is still there

But where to find the one who wants to care?

For when I look around, my eyes open wide

I see so few lights, have they gone to hide?

For reasons I ignore still

A fog has descended, to rob them of their will

To see the light that's sure there

But no one seems to be aware

Can it be extinguished through neglect

Or from disuse, its grown hard to detect

And what makes this even more severe

In its place he grown some fear

Fear of what, you might ask

Of almost everything, be it people or task

Masks have come to take its place

If worn too long, behind it will there be no face

For the light is that from which character grows

And the values one meets and knows

Things like courage, loyalty, ideals for which to strive

These are the things that keep us alive

Not just breathing, like some organism numb

No curious mind can succumb

For those who have abandoned themselves to darkness

Must renounce their light, though few confess

Blame is placed wherever it can

Spreading like some fog to woman and man

For the light illuminates one's personal core

Showing the way forward, indicating the door

To limit confusion, clarity bring

It's like winter ending to welcome the Spring

I see such ignorance among those who should know

Things aren't that complicated, their minds should grow

And when I question their reasons for choices they've made

They freeze for a moment, then seek to evade

For the truth belonging to one alone

Can show the place in their soul that once was home

It happened only quite recently

I met someone quite innocently

We spoke for awhile, exchanging thoughts

Thinking perhaps someone had actually learned what they were
taught

But soon discomfort started to appear

My questions found no answers, only fear

It was as if to ask, to know, was some sort of crime

He looked straight ahead, and for him that was fine

I saw the signs and knew what was next

He checked his phone as if he'd received a text

I pressed him, what was troubling him so

That he would choose not to know

Cornered, I could see the fear in him grow

The friendship he spoke of was lost below

And he turned it around, directing the blame at me

Claiming I spoke with too much "intensity"

I thought this odd for we think we all want clarity

Until such time as we have it, then can't stand to see

I know that my vision can burn when too close to the flame I go

I can keep what I see to myself for a time, but then I want to   know

If I must shut down so others can dance

I wonder if I do will I fall into the same trance

This cannot happen, I doubt I'd survive

How can one not know oneself, and still feel alive?

One sees this most clearly in the role of fantasy

Itscome to replace our sense of reality

I knew what he meant, a glimpse of himself he had seen

Not liking what he saw, as responsible, I had t o be mean

I asked what he feared, why did my words shake him so?

He stood up and let saying he had to go

I've found this with so many, to varying degrees

Not in my practice where the purpose one sees

But in contexts where masks must be worn

To remove it then, the illusion would be torn

The one, so addictive, worn every day

Never take it off or the price you'll pay

But which of the two prices, greater of less?

The one with "friends" where a few lies you might confess

Or the one, where the lies are those one tells to onself under no duress

I know which one – do you - is the costliest?

If we are born to be alive

To struggle, and win, and lose, and survive

Some may discover their truths and thrive

The others depend on their masks their identity to derive

Is our purpose here on this earth

More than just dying after giving birth?

To find one's path and follow it where it leads

Is this not the nourishment the Light itself needs

Failing this, the Light will grow weak

If this goes on too long, it will no longer speak

The embers may last a lifetime

But at the end of one's days, what will be left behind?

Of my time here, others to remind

To think well of me and to my memory be kind

Is that enough to face it all?

It's never too late to decide – just no longer stall

"As far as we can discern, the sole purpose of human existence is to kindle a light in the darkness of mere being"

C.G. Jung

ABOUT THE AUTHOR

Mitchell Ritter is a New York City born, Swiss trained clinical/Jungian psychologist. He spent many years living, studying and working in Europe, and has been back in New York since 2002. Living and working on the Upper East Side, he has two grown daughters and two large dogs.

For further information, please refer to the following website where the author provides insightful quotations and observations on current psychological and social issues drawn from his clinical practice:

www.analyticalpsychologynyc.com

and a website he runs where his interest in poetry finds a broad ranging expression.

www.amazon.com/ebooks/SixYears:AConcentrateofLife

Comments, thoughts, questions are all welcome and can be addressed to:

analyticalpsychologynyc@gmail.com

- **MR. HIDE'S PROGRESS** – A parable about why people make the wrong choices

- **SIX YEARS – A CONCENTRATE OF LIFE** – A Collection – Volume I